Educational Child's Play
Play Based Child Development Activities
Prepare children emotionally, intellectually and physically,
before they start school.

Written and illustrated by Paul Mackie.
cover graphic by olga1818 shutterstock.com

Library and Archives Canada Cataloguing in Publication

Mackie, Paul, 1951-, author
Educational child's play / Paul Mackie.

ISBN 978-0-9809490-0-1 (softcover)

1. Play. 2. Early childhood education--Activity programs.
3. Activity programs in education. 4. Day care centers--Activity
programs. I. Title.

LB1140.35.P55M33 2017   372.21   C2017-901016-6

Copyright© 2017 by Paul Mackie
http://howtoteachchildrentoread.ca

All rights reserved. No part of this book may be reproduced, or utilized in any form, or by any means, electronic, mechanical or photocopying (unless stated in this book), without permission in writing from the Author.
Storybook pages are black and white and can be copied for children to color.

Contents

- DEDICATION 5
- THIS BOOK IN A NUTSHELL 6
- DISCLAIMER 7
- "A WALK IN THE JUNGLE" STORYBOOK 9
- USING PUPPETS IN YOUR STORY 42
- TIPS WHEN USING PUPPETS IN YOUR STORY 48
- "GORDY VISITS THE MOUNTAINS" 53
- HOW TO DO THE STORY'S MOVEMENTS 82
- TEACHING TIPS 84
- MATERIALS TO ENHANCE THE STORY 86
- GORDY VISITS THE MOUNTAINS STORY MAT 88
- MOVING TO RELAX 95
- SOME POSSIBILITIES 96
- FRIENDLY WAVE 97
- LISTENING EARS 98
- WATER 99
- ENERGY BOOST 100
- CROSSOVERS 101
- CONNECTIONS 102
- BACK ARCH 103
- MASSAGE YAWN 104
- TENSION AND RELEASE 105
- VISUALIZATION 106
- THE BALANCE BOARD 108
- THINGS WE CAN DO ON THE BALANCE BOARD 109
- BALANCE BOARD ACTIVITIES 110
- PASS THE STICK OVER YOUR SHOULDER 111
- THROW KOOSH BALL AT A TARGET 112
- THE ADJUSTABLE BALANCE BOARD 113
- HOW TO MAKE THE BALANCE BOARD 114
- HOW TO MAKE THE ROTATIONAL BALANCE BOARD 115
- THE SENSORY ENVIRONMENT 118
- SENSORY ENVIRONMENTS WHY? WHAT? WHERE? AND HOW TO DO IT? 123
- CREATING A DARK PLANET ROOM 124
- SENSORY ENVIRONMENTS VESTIBULAR ACTIVITIES 128
- VESTIBULAR ACTIVITIES 129
- PROPRIOCEPTIVE ACTIVITIES 130

FUN DAY ACTIVITIES INTRODUCTION	156
BUBBLE DIAGRAMS	157
BOOKS	158
BOWLING	159
CITY TRANSIT	160
CARNIVAL RIDES	161
CHILDREN	162
CHINESE CULTURE	163
CLEANING	164
CLOWNING AROUND	165
COLORING	166
COMMUNITY	167
COMPUTERS	168
DANCING	169
DENTIST	170
DRAWING	171
FLOWERS	172
FOOD	173
HELPING OTHERS	174
HORSES	175
JEWELRY	176
LEADERSHIP AND YOUR LEGACY	177
LIBRARY	178
MONEY	179
MOVIES	180
MUSIC	181
NEEDLEWORK	182
OUTDOORS	183
PAINTING	184
PAPER SHREDDING	185
PARKS	186
PEOPLE WATCHING	187
PIANO	188
PLANTS AND FLOWERS	189
PRINTING	190
PUZZLES	191
READING	192
RECYCLING	193
RIDING IN VEHICLES	194

SCRAPBOOKING	195
SHOPPING	196
SOCCER	197
SOCIALIZING	198
TRUCKS	199
WATER ACTIVITIES	200
CONNECTING WITH OUR PLANET - MOTHER NATURE	201
CONNECTING CHILDREN WITH MOTHER NATURE	202
BENEFITS OF GROWING AND GARDENING	203
HOW TO DEAL WITH CHILDREN'S BEHAIORS	206
A METHOD TO DEAL WITH MOST CHILDREN'S BEHAVIORS	208
AVOIDING BURN OUT	209
SOME COMMON BEHAVIORS IN PRE-SCHOOL CHILDREN	210
WHAT HAPPENS WHEN NONE OF THIS WORKS?	212
DEALING WITH EMOTIONS	215
ANGRY FACE	218
CALM FACE	219
HURT FACE	220
WELL FACE	221
BASIC SIGN LANGUAGE - YES	222
BASIC SIGN LANGUAGE - NO	223
BASIC SIGN LANGUAGE - STOP	224
BASIC SIGN LANGUAGE - BATHROOM - TOILET	225
BASIC SIGN LANGUAGE – STORY TIME	226
BASIC SIGN LANGUAGE – EAT - HUNGRY	227
Basic Sign Language – SLEEP - NAP TIME	228
FOR THOSE THAT WANT TO KNOW MORE	229
WHAT CAN EDUCATIONAL CHILD'S PLAY DO FOR A CHILD?	230
FROM THE ONTARIO EARLY YEARS FRAMEWORK REPORT	231
OTHER BOOKS BY THE AUTHOR	232
BIBLIOGRAPHY	235
ABOUT THE AUTHOR	236

DEDICATION

This book is dedicated to helping pre-school children from the ages of birth to six years of age be the best that they can be.

To achieve that, this book has TWO DEVELOPMENTAL STORIES:
A Walk In The Jungle - a story to help children develop cognitive, behavioral, emotional and motor skills.

Gordy Visits The Mountains - a story that uses play based movements to develop pre-school children.

PLAY BASED ACTIVITIES:

Play based activities - That scientists are saying children need in the first seven years of life.

The sensory environment - Setting up the environment to develop seven senses. Sensory environments can enhance learning and cognitive growth.

Using puppets in your stories - Gets children actively involved in the stories and activities.

Fun Day Activities - Thousands of activities for children to try, or to be discussed.

ESSENTIAL KNOWLEDGE FOR ANY PARENT OR CAREGIVER:

How To Deal With Children's Behaviors - Developmental milestones and how to deal with the behaviors that accompany them.

Moving To Relax - is the same movements as in the Developmental Stories, but in adult form.

The storybook movements are demonstrated here:
https://youtu.be/lGFxfKjOYHI

For Those That Want To Know More - This section of the book explains the benefits of the book's activities in more depth.

Contact the author: educationalchildsplay@gmail.com

THIS BOOK IN A NUTSHELL

non stimulated brain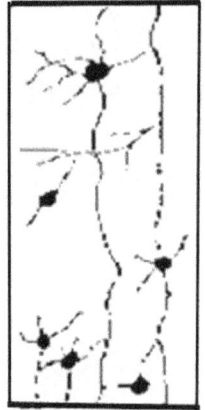
fewer pathways to enable thought development

stimulated brain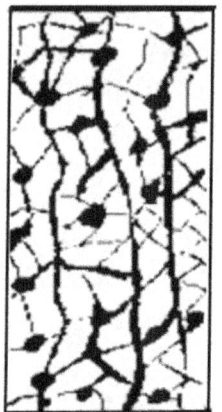
a rich network of pathways to permit complex thinking

Give a pre-school child from birth to six years of age an UNPRECEDENTED, LIFELONG advantage; simply by using Educational Child's Play to stimulate their brain.

A book that provides fun play-based pre-school child development activities when a child needs them, in the early years from birth to six years of age.

THIS BOOK IS FOR: parents, pre-school teachers, Early Childhood Educators, Day Cares, and anyone who wants children to be the best that they can be.

Simple things like reading and telling stories to a child at 18 months; or joining a three-year-old child to play with a bucket and sand; or helping a four-year-old throw a ball in the playground, are powerful stimuli for brain development in the early years. These activities are laying the foundation of brain development for future learning, behavior and health.

This book provides pre-school children with what science is saying they need in the early years, simply by reading them the stories, and using the play-based activities in Educational Child's Play.

DISCLAIMER

Note: It is advisable to consult a doctor before beginning any exercise program. The author offers the information and movements in this book only when advised by a doctor to do so and does not accept any responsibility for its misuse.

The suggested movements are adaptations of several programs, methods and techniques that are listed in the reference section of this book. In no way do they represent the potential, methods or techniques of those programs.
The author's claims are based on benefits to himself and of children in his care and the activity benefits listed may help with but are not guaranteed or proven results.

AGE APPROPRIATNESS
The activities in this book are for children from birth to six years of age; as well as having the same potential benefits for adult caregivers or teachers.

The Developmental Stories are generally for children aged 2 years or older but can be read to younger children; if younger children will allow it, the activity movements can be done by the caregiver for the child; or hand over hand.

COMMENTS:
"A Walk In The Jungle" has been a successful addition to our classrooms.
It has been a wonderful and fun way to calm our children and ready them for daily transitions.
J White-Program Director.

"Gordy Visits The Mountains" has been extremely beneficial to my daughter's development. Being born with no binocular vision had a large impact on her gross motor development. My daughter loves to practice all the time with the gross motor equipment in this fun story setting. Now, six months later, her gross motor skills are right at age level and she's always excited to have the chance to practice her new-found skills on the equipment.
J White-Parent

Paul Mackie's remarkable book takes children through beneficial exercises in a fun and playful way. Children stay focused as they participate in each page of the story and can use their own imaginations as they follow the delightful story characters. What a great way for children to begin their day.
Rose Berzai-Parent

I use Paul's book in a home-based program with a six year old boy who is autistic. The boy laughs, enjoys himself, seems to be more focused and able to concentrate after the storybook exercises. Another good thing is that the exercises are transferable to different environments and can be done anywhere.
Emily Walsh-Special Education Assistant

"A WALK IN THE JUNGLE" STORYBOOK

An activity story to calm, relax and enhance a child's learning.

Some possibilities for children 2 years or older:

☺ increased self-esteem.
☺ increased self-control.
☺ calms and relaxes children and adults.
☺ creates a calm and relaxed environment.
☺ overcomes learning stress.
☺ makes changes in routine easier.
☺ helps children be more self directing.
☺ empowers parents and teachers to make a difference in their children's growth.

A Walk In the Jungle is a storybook with a purpose. The story includes activities and movements to help children and adults reduce daily stress, enhance learning, and above all have fun while playing.

The above lists some of the benefits the author has observed in himself and children under his care. The movements are adaptations from several personal development and stress reduction methods the author has experienced and used successfully with children over several years.

The black and white pictures can be copied and colored by both adult and child to provide a relaxing or cooperative parent/child experience.
Remember, it's ok to color outside the lines! It is not the final picture that counts but the quality shared time and experience that your child will remember long after this book has gone.

For ease of presentation to children, the following storybooks can be purchased at:
http://www.lulu.com/spotlight/paulmackie

I cannot guarantee results by practicing any of the activities in this book. The benefits listed are purely anecdotal, based on observed benefits to myself and others in my care.
I suggest you try them. It is my hope that they work for you, as they did for me.

"Hi boys and girls. I am Nellie the elephant.

Let's put on our listening ears."

Listening Ears

May help with: Listening and focusing skills.

Why it is important: This activity has several purposes. It takes attention away from play and other activities while getting the children to focus and listen.
This method is used in kinesiology and acupressure to help with short term memory, listening skills and language skills.

How it is done: Grasp each ear with the thumb on the inside rim and the pointer finger on the outside rim. Uncurl the ear down to the ear lobe using the pointer finger along with the thumb. Bring pointer finger and thumb back to the top of the ear and repeat several times.

Nellie is waving at us with her trunk.

She wants us to join her for a walk in the jungle.

Put out your trunk and wave to Nellie.

Now wave with your other trunk.

Elephant Wave

May help with: Listening, balance and memory.

Why it is important: This movement acknowledges the children's presence in a friendly way and May help with listening comprehension, auditory memory and sense of balance. Developing the ability to listen, retain information and have whole body co-ordination, are essential skills for easy learning, and good social interaction with peers.

How it is done: Tilt your head, placing your ear on the shoulder while extending your arm forward. With your hand draw an infinity sign (an 8 on its side) the width of your shoulders, focusing your eyes beyond the finger tips. Your body and arm move as one unit with no twisting at the hips.
Do several times with each arm.

Nellie is going for a walk in the jungle, but the sun is so bright Nellie has to close her eyes; Close your eyes; let us be the sun.

What colour are you?
What shape are you?
How do you feel?
Are you cold or hot?

Visualization

May help with: Visualization and problem solving.

Why it is important: This helps children to use the right hemisphere of the brain (usually the creative side in most people). This activity teaches children how to solve problems by picturing what is going on. It is best to use visualization images from the environment.
Being able to picture what is going on in the mind's eye is an important skill in problem solving.

How it is done: Ask the children to close their eyes and imagine the sun as various colors, shapes and sizes.
Ask about feelings.
          Remember, there are no wrong answers.

Nellie is getting thirsty because it is so hot.

She sees a cool clear pool of water and stops to take a drink.

Let's have a drink of water just like Nellie.

Water

May help with: Learning and energy levels.

Why it is important: Water assists learning and thought. Water helps us store and retrieve information, improves energy levels, improves mental and physical
coordination. Water helps conduct the electrical and chemical processes of the brain for clear thinking.

How it is done: Having a water bottle close by is an easy way to take a drink during the story.

Here comes one of Nellie's friends, Gordy the gorilla.

Look! he is doing his gorilla talk.

Let's all do our gorilla talk.

Let's make some gorilla noises.

Gorilla Talk

May help with: Increased energy and relaxation.

Why it is important: Being relaxed and energetic makes learning easier. Massaging the kidney 27s pressure points increases energy levels, relaxes the body, and helps both sides of the brain work together.

How it is done: Place your hand on your neck (palm on the Adam's apple) with thumb on one side and fingers on the other. Move your hand down until you feel your collar- bone, jump over it and massage the soft spots between the next set of ribs and the collarbone. Place your other hand on your belly button (do not massage with this hand).
Switch both hands and repeat for about 30 seconds.

Here come some monkey friends; see how they do the monkey walk.

Let's all do our monkey walk.

Let's make some monkey noises.

Monkey Walk

May help with: Accessing the whole brain.

Why it is important: Using both sides of the brain is essential for reading, comprehension and body coordination. This cross over movement activates both brain hemispheres simultaneously, increases whole body coordination, improves fitness and spatial awareness.

How it is done: Lift your left leg and touch your left knee with your right hand.
Put the foot down and lift your right leg and touch your right knee with your left hand.
Repeat three or more times.
Children having difficulty can match colored bands, gloves or stickers placed on opposite hands and knees.

There's Freddy the frog!
He's lying on a lily pad.
Let's all lie like Freddy on our lily pads.
Let's make some frog noises.
Let's do some frog jumping.

Resting Frog

May help with: De-stressing and easier learning.

Why it is important: Being relaxed and focused helps make learning easier and improves self-esteem. This cross over movement is helpful to de-stress the mind and body, to increase attention, counterbalance negative thoughts and feelings and may improve self-esteem.

How it is done: Can be done sitting or lying down. Ask the children to lie on the floor, cross their feet at the ankles and give themselves a big hug by placing their hands under each arm pit.

The heat is making Nellie tired.

Look how she is yawning.

Let's all do a big elephant yawn just like Nellie.

Elephant Yawn

May help with: Speaking and increased energy.

Why it is important: Having more energy, a relaxed jaw and facial muscles makes it easier for children to think clearly, communicate, sing and express themselves. Massage and yawning improves energy to the brain; may help with public speaking; relaxes vision and clears thinking.

How it is done: Children take a deep breath and yawn.
A yawning or elephant sound can be made.

Nellie wants to rest in the shade of some trees.

Let's all be trees and make some shade for Nellie.

Reach your branches up to the sky.

Resting Trees

May help with: Visualization and imagination.

Why it is important: Being able to imagine and picture in the mind's eye is an essential problem solving skill. This movement uses visualization and imagination and teaches children how to tense and relax the body.

How it is done: Ask children to imagine they are trees. Put your arms straight up and spread the fingers wide.

You are all big strong trees, so reach up high, reach your branches to the sky.

Now push your feet (your roots) hard into the ground.

Reach high and push.

Here comes the wind!

Let's be the wind.

Resting trees

May help with: Relaxation and body control.

Why it is important: The movement teaches children how to use tension and release to gain body control and relax.

How it is done: Reach straight up as high as you can. Spread your fingers (branches) wide and push your feet (roots) down to the ground. Push and reach together; this puts the body into tension. Sway (wind) from one foot to the other; this releases tension. Repeat several times.

Now it's getting dark. Our branches are resting.

Let our branches hang down to the ground to rest.

Resting trees

May help with: Relaxation and calming.

Why it is important: This movement calms and readies children for the next activity.

How it is done: Bend forward and let the arms hang loosely down to the ground.

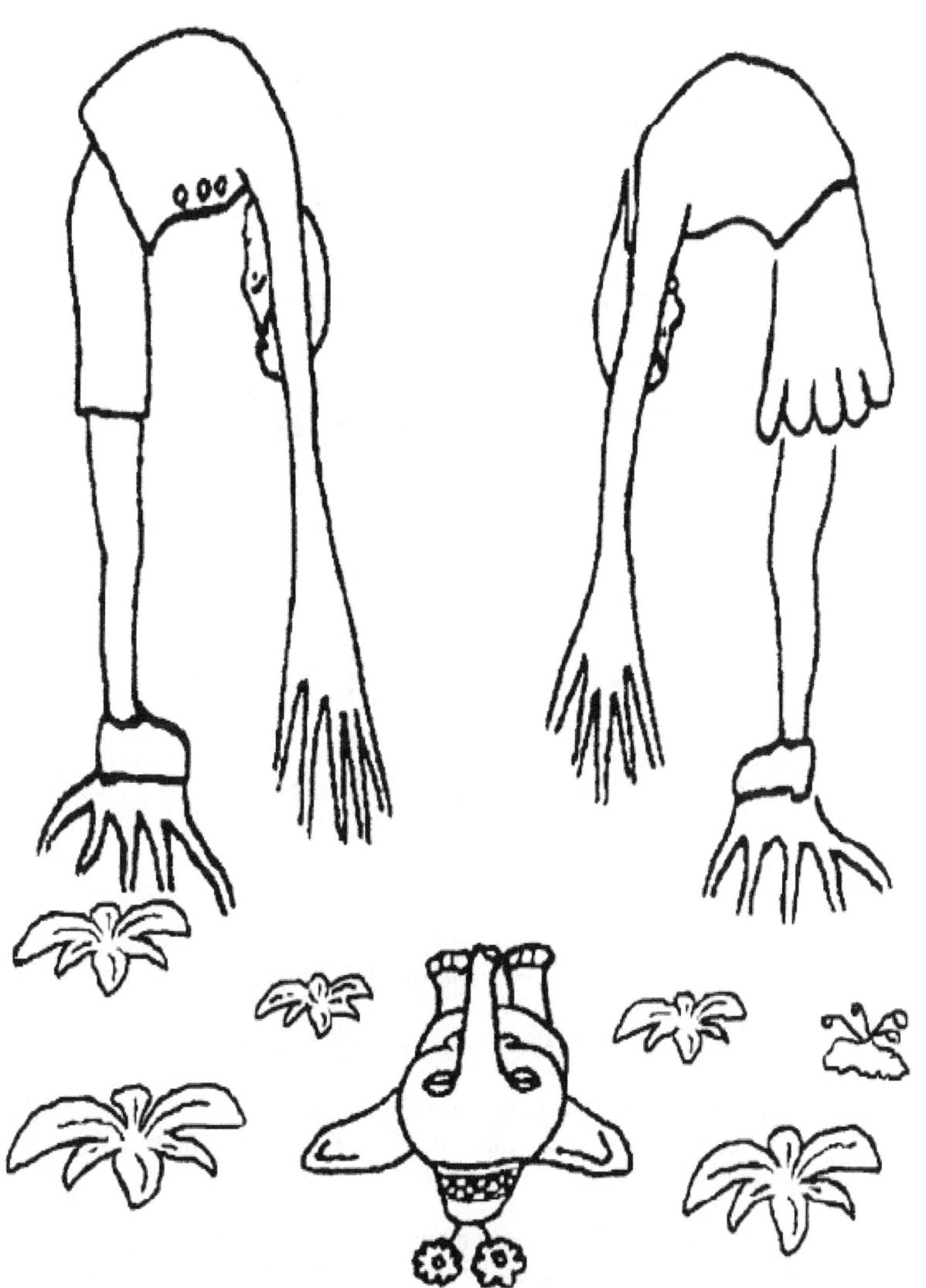

Close your eyes.
Nellie can see the bright moon coming up.

You are the moon.

Open your eyes and make a moon with your fingers; reach up high with your moon in the sky.

What shape is your moon?

Visualize The Moon

May help with: Visualization, shapes and communication.

Why it is important: Being able to imagine and picture in the mind's eye is an essential problem solving skill. Providing opportunities to express and verbalize such images is also essential.

How it is done: From the bending position form a moon by placing the tips of the fingers together. Raise the arms until the hands are above the head, arch the back slightly and look through the circle formed by the fingers.

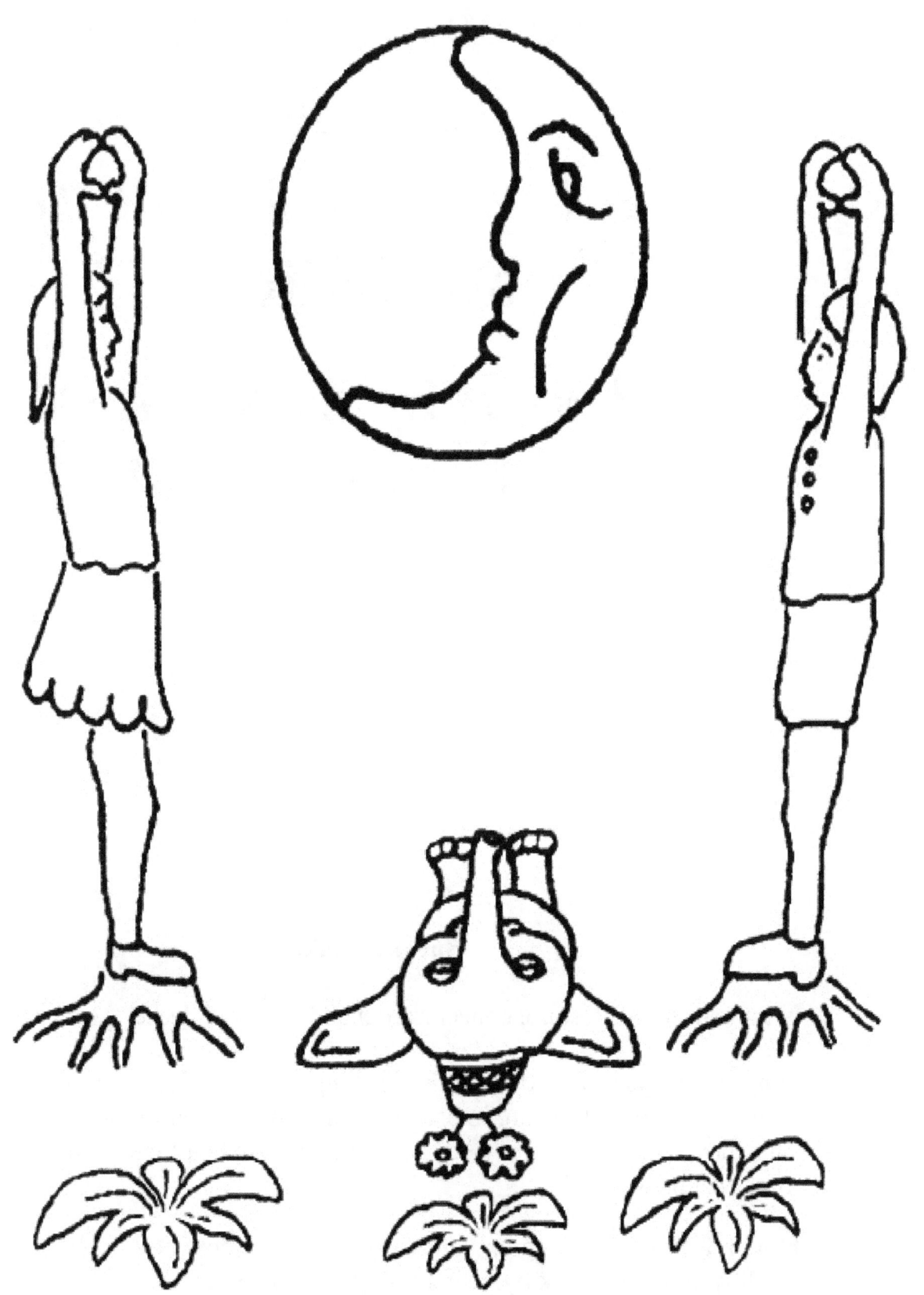

Here comes Sammy the snake; he is trying to sneak up on Nellie.

Let's all be ssssnakes. Wake up Nellie!

Sneaky Snake

May help with: Posture, concentration and tension release.

Why it is important: After sitting for long periods, slightly arching the back helps release body tension, improve posture and concentration.
This movement helps relax body tension, increase hand-eye coordination and improve posture.

How it is done: Resting on your elbows, lie face down on the floor.
Slightly arch your back by lifting your head backwards.
Relax by bringing your head down. Repeat several times.

Here comes Leo the lion.

He's full of energy after his nap.

Let's all roar with Leo.

What other animals would we see in the jungle?

Let's be different animals. How would we move?

Leo the Lion Roar

May help with: Energy and verbal expression.

Why it is important: Having more energy, a relaxed jaw and facial muscles make it easier for children to think clearly, communicate and sing.
The roaring sound helps children express themselves. The same movement as the elephant yawn.

How it is done: Put your fingers on your cheeks. Find the pivotal points of the jaw by opening and closing the jaw. While yawning, massage the points with the fingers. A yawning or roaring lion sound can be made.

Well, boys and girls, it's time for Nellie to go back home.

Nellie says thank you; she had fun with you on her jungle walk.

Wave goodbye; goodbye Nellie!

See you tomorrow.

Elephant Wave

May help with: listening, balance and memory.

Why it is important: Developing the ability to listen, retain information, and have whole body co-ordination, are essential skills for easy learning, and good social interaction with peers.

How it is done: Tilt your head, placing your ear on the shoulder while extending your arm forward. With your hand draw an infinity sign (an 8 on its side) the width of your shoulders, focusing your eyes beyond the finger - tips. Your body and arm move as one unit, with no twisting at the hips. Do several times with each arm.

Ask the children to pick an animal from the "Walk In The Jungle" story, and to be that animal.

Free expression

As with all the movements the children are free to express themselves. Usually the children will watch you and try to copy your movements. With this page **you do not demonstrate,** instead you help the children talk about and act out animals of their choice.

The story closure: at this point transition the children to other activities by using an animal stamp (dollar stores usually have the ones that light up) or an animal puppet.

You can also transition the children to another activity by doing the Monkey Walk.

A WALK IN THE JUNGLE
"using puppets in your story"

USING PUPPETS IN YOUR STORY

A WALK IN THE JUNGLE

I stumbled across the use of puppets in my story telling after a friend gave me a puppet that reminded him of the elephant character in my storybook,
"A Walk in the Jungle"; Nellie the elephant was born.

The children took to the puppet immediately, and I was surprised by some of the things that children would do and say to the puppet, that they would not do, or say to an adult.

Before I explain how to use the puppets in your story, first let me introduce the six characters and their use in my storybooks.

Nellie the elephant - the main character:

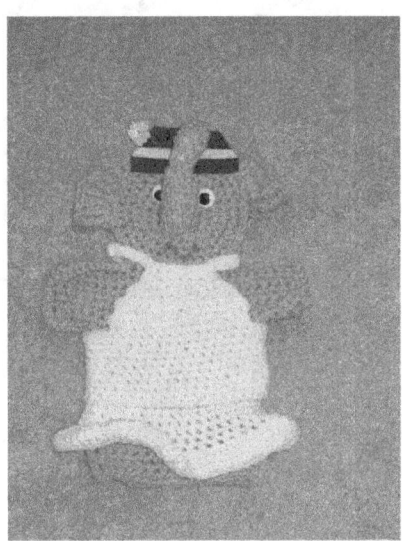

Nellie the elephant is the main character in the storybook, "A Walk in the Jungle" at:

http://www.lulu.com/spotlight/paulmackie

The above picture shows a knitted puppet 12 inches long and 8 inches wide at the arms, this fits a hand about 4 inches wide by 7 inches long; all the knitted character are approximately this size. The puppets can be made from colored felt quite easily, but they are not as durable, are less attractive and huggable (more about this later) to the children.

My preference is the knitted puppet, which is more expensive to produce, but overall is worth the effort, in both my personal feelings and resulting benefits for the children. Nellie is associated with the movement called the "Elephant Wave" which can help with sense of balance and acknowledges the children's presence.

The next character is:

Gordy the Gorilla – main character in the storybook, "Gordy Visits The Mountains".
At: **http://www.lulu.com/spotlight/paulmackie**

Gordy is associated with the movement called "Gorilla Talk".

This movement is based on an acupressure technique that is said to increase energy and help use both sides of the Brain at the same time. This movement can energize the children and help them use more of the Brain's potential. Let me just point out that all the benefits I mention are purely anecdotal and from personal observation.
The Gordy gorilla puppet and the gorilla talk movement can be used to transition children from one activity to another.
Initially I used the large puppet for this purpose, but found that a small finger puppet held the children's attention in the same way.
To get children to re-direct, I would bring out the puppet and say, "let's put on our listening ears" (see "A Walk in the Jungle storybook"), then I would say "Let's do our gorilla talk as we go to wash our hands".
It is good practice to allow the children time to process what you are asking them to do.
Take the time to interact with the children, using the puppet as a real person works well with children (more about that later).

The next character is:

Mickey The Monkey.

The monkey is associated with the movement called "The Monkey Walk"

This movement is a cross lateral movement and May help with using both sides of the brain at the same time, body and hand eye coordination.
This movement can be difficult for children as you are asking them to do two things at once i.e. lift their left leg and touch it with their right hand (generally, the left Brain governs the right side of the body and the right Brain the left side of the body). Matching colored bands on legs and hands can be used to help with this movement.
The Monkey Walk is also a transitional activity, and when accompanied by some monkey talking ("eeee, eeee, eeee) is extremely effective.
This character is in a later storybook about learning to read and is also in the storybook "A Walk in the Jungle".

The next character is:

Freddy the Frog

Freddy the frog is associated with the movement called "Resting Frog"

Being relaxed and focused makes learning easier.
The resting frog movement is done by asking the children to lie on the floor, cross their ankles and put their hands under their armpits (see "A Walk In The Jungle storybook").

Freddy can also be used to help children express themselves. This is usually done by asking the children, "Can Freddy give you a hug?" and following up with a question, or addressing a concern i.e. "Freddy can see that you are sad, why is that?"

Hugging can be beneficial to preschool children. Children usually wrap their arms around the puppet and may even pinch or nip the puppet. Always ask permission to hug a child; and address any of the child's behavior that is not acceptable.

The next character is:

Sammy The Snake

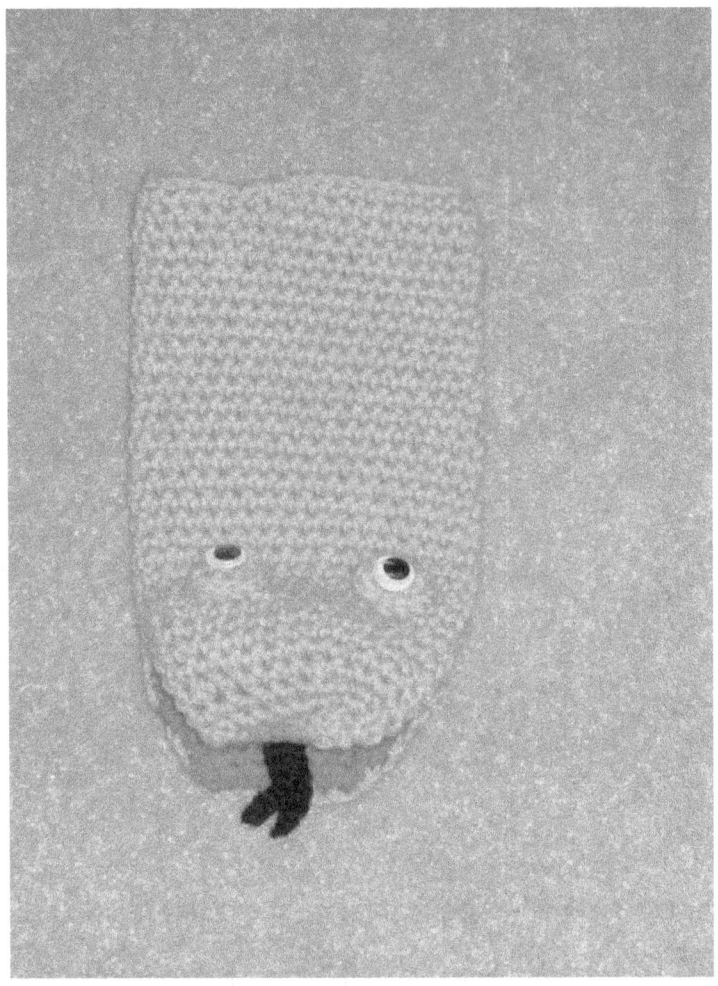

Sammy The Snake is associated with the movement called "Sneaky Snake".

This movement is like some Yoga postures and is used to help relax body tension and improve posture.
With this movement I get the children to pretend they are snakes, sneaking up on Nellie the elephant, then, get them to shout at the top of their voices, "wake up Nellie".
All the activities in the story can be added to by asking a further question, such as, "What other things do snakes do?"

A good point to mention is that there are no wrong answers and that it is best to let the children express themselves freely. As the story teller you are always consistent with the way you present the story; the children will notice if you are not.

The final character is:

Leo The Lion

Leo The Lion is associated with the movement called "Leo The Lion Roar".

The lion roar May help with energy a verbal expression. I personally use this movement if I am going to do any public speaking, it helps relax the jaw and makes speaking more fluent.

With children, it generally helps to express themselves by roaring like a lion, and any other sound the lion might make.

TIPS WHEN USING PUPPETS IN YOUR STORY

To get the story started, I usually hide the puppet under my sweater and pretend that Nellie is having a nap; I then ask the children to wake Nellie up by shouting "wake up!"
The children usually take three tries to get Nellie to wake up, the last try being the loudest.
Once Nellie wakes up, I usually yawn and explain that I was having a nap, at this point you are speaking as the puppet; do not disguise your voice. It is amazing that the children will distinguish a difference between you and the puppet, regardless of how your voice sounds.

On one occasion I was doing a circle story time with a group of children and asked if anyone would like to give Nellie a hug. One five year old boy came up and hugged Nellie; he then asked Nellie if he could tell her a secret; I whispered "Yes". The boy whispered the secret in the puppet's ear and then said, "Don't tell Paul". I did hear the secret as he whispered, and commented by saying, "Did you tell Nellie your secret?"
This sort of thing never ceases to amaze me, it is my belief that children, usually under five years old, do not see a difference between the puppet and the puppeteer.

Another interesting point is that children see the puppet as real.
I was just finishing a story with a group of children and was clearing my story props away when I picked up the Nellie puppet and threw it in a box. The children gasped and said, "Oh Nellie!" I quickly realized what I had done and retrieved the puppet saying how sorry I was to the puppet. I placed the puppet on my hand and had Nellie say that she was "ok". I always end a story by having Nellie say she is going to have a nap, and lay the puppet gently on the ground, or back inside my sweater.
Never mistreat the puppet!

I always clear away my puppets, so that the children are not able to access them; I find that this maintains the illusion of a real character.

As mentioned earlier, the puppets can be made of different materials and be of different sizes. Usually I carry a finger puppet in my pocket, so that I can engage the children in an activity or transition them to another activity. This technique works very well, and in most cases the children will respond to the puppet's lead.

On one occasion I was using Nellie the elephant to transition some children to the bathroom; one child came up and pulled hard on Nellie's trunk.
Knowing that this would have hurt a real person, I said "Ow! That hurt". I then told the child that Nellie was hurt and how could we make her feel better.
The child hugged the puppet and walked away to the bathroom. This is another interesting phenomenon; children will pinch or try to hurt the puppet.
I usually respond as any real person would, and then address the situation on the puppets behalf. It is not difficult to jump from one role as yourself and one as the puppet character.
These are a few pictures of the storybook character finger puppets. One set of puppets is made from felt, and the other set is knitted.

Just to recap

Children will:

- say things to the puppet but will not say them to you.
- tell the puppet secrets, and express how they are feeling to the puppet, but not to you.
- associate the puppet with its movement, or role in the story.
- see the puppet as a real person, or character.
- will try to hurt the puppet, at times.
- will hug and show affection to the puppet, but sometimes not to you.
- be upset if you mistreat the puppet.
- express themselves, if the puppet asks them to.
- notice any inconsistencies in your story presentation.
- be more confident, and not be shy around the puppet.

Always:

- allow children time to transition from one activity to another.
- be consistent in how you present the puppet movements and story.
- treat the puppet with gentle, tender care.
- ask the children first, if it is ok to do something, or make changes.
- be honest about how you and the puppet are feeling.
- address any abuse of the puppet as you would a real situation.

"Gordy Visits The Mountains"
How to: use movement to develop a child

"GORDY VISITS THE MOUNTAINS"

How to use movement to develop a child; for children 2 - 6 years of age

Studies and the works of some authors have shown that certain movements are a necessary part of a child's development for both mind and body (the balanced child). This book introduces some of those movements in a simple and play-based story.

The purpose of the book is to provide children up to the age of 6 years with a fun, creative movement activity that can become self-directing.

The benefits of the story can be improvements in:

- **social behavior**
- **physical coordination**
- **self-direction**
- **sequential processing (for reading, math, alphabet etc.)**
- **creative child involvement**
- **independent choices**
- **imagination**
- **self-esteem**
- **confidence, sensitivity, caring and sharing attitude.**

For example, it has been the author's experience to have children ask for this book in order to act out the story with their peers and friends; to see older children (of their own accord) use the story to instruct the younger children; to have children who are normally passive participate and express themselves. In other words, the benefits are the natural results of the children's own development.

It is the author's hope that you will use the stories "A Walk In The Jungle" and "Gordy Visits The Mountains" to prove for yourself that the benefits listed are achievable. If nothing else, above all, have FUN and play with your children!

Hi! Boys and girls. My name is Gordy the gorilla. Let's put on our listening ears ...just like Gordy!

May help with: Listening and focusing skills.

Why it is important: Attention is taken away from play and other activities while getting children to focus and listen.

How it is done: Grasp each ear with the thumb on the inside rim and the pointer finger on the outside rim.

Uncurl the ear down to the ear lobe using the pointer finger along with the thumb.

Bring pointer finger and thumb back to the top of the ear and repeat several times.

Today, Gordy is going to walk to his mountain friends for a visit.

Let's do some gorilla walking by hopping from one foot to the other...just like Gordy!

What other ways can we do some gorilla walking? What other ways can we jump and hop?

May help with: Whole body coordination.

Why it is important: Using both sides of the body at the same time, develops postural control and whole body coordination.

How it is done: Hop from one foot to the other with arms slightly out to the sides.

Ask children to show you other ways to hop; try not to prompt them.

Gordy comes to a flowing river.
Luckily there is a tree that has fallen across it.
Gordy balances slowly on the fallen tree to the other side of the river.
Let's all balance on the fallen tree and cross the river ...just like Gordy!

May help with: Balance, awareness of gravity and space.

Why it is important: Sequential movement may help with basic math, logic and reasoning skills. This movement helps the child develop an awareness of both sides of the body, gravity, space and balance. Use of both brain hemispheres as well as the development of the vestibular system can make learning easier.

How it is done: Walk slowly over the balance beam (a piece of sanded smooth wood 1"x 6") by placing one foot in front of the other (heel to toe). Hold the hands of unsteady children if necessary. If the children are confident then walk backwards.

Gordy steps off the tree onto some laughing rocks. The laughing rocks start giggling as Gordy's feet tickle their heads. This makes Gordy laugh. Let's all walk on the rocks and laugh… just like Gordy! What other ways can we make people laugh?

May help with: Balance, feeling of laughter and joy.

Why it is important: Balancing helps develop the vestibular system and balance making it easier to learn. Laughter and joy promote a feeling of happiness and reduces stressful situations.

How it is done: As the children walk on the rocks ask them to laugh. Demonstrate by laughing yourself. Be as natural as Possible.
Use joke books and funny situations.

Gordy sees a giant rock with a big tunnel hole through it. Let's all crawl through the tunnel rock… just like Gordy! What other ways can we crawl? What animals crawl? Let's be a crawling animal.

May help with: Using both sides of the brain together.

Why it is important: Crawling is a basic developmental stage which has a bilateral movement (the opposite arm and leg work together). Crawling leads to being able to use both sides of the brain together and develops physical skills to help children learn how to read and write.

How it is done: The children crawl through a tunnel or under a table. Entice the children through by waiting on the other side of the tunnel (encouraging them to come to you); give lots of praise.

Gordy comes across another fallen tree on the path.
He swings both his arms and jumps over it with both feet.
Let's all jump over the fallen tree… just like Gordy!
What animals jump with two feet?
Let's be those animals and jump.

May help with: Equal use of both sides of the body.

Why it is important: Lifting the whole body vertically off the ground demonstrates children's whole body coordination, and an awareness of their relationship to space.

How it is done: Both arms and knees swing up together, as you raise your feet off the ground and move forward. The children jump over the balance tree.

Oh oh! Gordy steps on a thorn with his foot. Look how he is hopping! Let's all hop on one foot … just like Gordy! What sort of noises would Gordy be making? How would he be feeling?

May help with: Postural control of the whole body.

Why it is important: Hopping helps to gain postural control of the whole body and awareness of the shift in gravity as the child moves.

How it is done: Generally, toddlers will not be able to hop on one foot. To assist the children have them hold onto the back of a chair and jump on one foot. Three to five year olds will be able to hop 3 to 10 hops.

Try hopscotch games.

Gordy sits down in a bed of flowers and removes the thorn from his foot. Sniff, sniff! Gordy smells the flowers. Let's smell the flowers … just like Gordy! What do the flowers smell like? What colors are they?

May help with: Calming and relaxing.

Why it is important: Smell is our most acute sense. Use Lavender and Chamomile to relax.

How it is done: Add a few drops of essential oil to some cotton balls or felt flowers and have the children guess the smell.
Have pictures of the different smells to show children.

Here comes the rain to make the flowers grow. Gordy grows just like the flowers. He reaches up with his arms and pushes with his feet. Let's all reach up with our arms, push with our feet and grow strong, just like Gordy! What other things grow? Let's be some of those things.

May help with: Body control and relaxation.

Why it is important: Teaches how to use tension and release to gain body control and relax.

How it is done: Have the children reach up with both arms then ask them to push with their feet (the feet should not rise off the floor-just like pushing a spike into the ground with your heel).

Here comes the wind. It blows Gordy around and around.

Let's spin around ... just like Gordy! Let's be the wind. How would it blow?

May help with: Balance and easier learning.

Why it is important: Spinning is said to improve children's learning abilities by moving fluid inside the inner ear, thus improving coordination and the vestibular system.

How it is done: You spin both ways three times with your arms outstretched. For older children use a rotational balance board (two circular boards with a bearing between them that can spin as the child sits on it).

 SAFETY TIP: Some children with brain dysfunction may be prone to seizures and should not spin or be spun around; always consult a doctor for children with special needs.
Spinning may reduce breathing and blood pressure which may cause loss of consciousness.

The wind spins Gordy to his mountain friends.
They are happy to see him.
Gordy gives his mountain friends a big hug.
Let's hug our friends … just like Gordy!
What other ways do we greet or say hello to our friends?

May help with: Stress reduction and increased happiness.

Why it is important: Hugging is said to provide a sense of companionship and happiness; reduce stress and improve the quality of life.

How it is done: Ask the children to find someone to hug, or they can hug Gordy the puppet or you. After reading the story a few times it is interesting to note that children will automatically find someone to hug as soon as you turn the page.

Gordy's mountain friends ask him to play balance ball.
Gordy stands on one leg and throws the bean bag at the hoop.
Let's balance and throw the bean bag ... just like Gordy!
Can you throw the bean bag with your other hand?

May help with: Body balance and hand/eye coordination.

Why it is important: : Balancing develops learning through the vestibular and sensory systems.
Throwing and balancing is said to develop a bigger brain.

How it is done: Stand on one leg, throw with one hand then the other hand.

Here comes Gordy's friend Mickey the monkey. They are going to play balance catch. Let's play balance catch ... just like Gordy and Mickey! Pass and catch with your other hand.

May help with: Coordination skills and teamwork.

Why it is important: Balancing and catching develop hand/eye and physical coordination skills. Working with a partner develops teamwork, self-direction and social skills.

How it is done: Stand on one leg, throw with one hand then the other hand; take turns throwing.

Gordy is using his gorilla talk to say goodbye.
Let's use our gorilla talk and say goodbye
… just like Gordy!
Let's make some gorilla noises.
Bye Gordy. Bye-bye!

May help with: Increased energy and relaxation.

Why it is important: Being relaxed and energetic makes learning easier.

How it is done: Place your hand on your neck (palm on the Adam's apple) with thumb on one side and fingers on the other. Move your hand down until you feel your collar bone, jump over it and massage the soft spots between the next set of ribs and the collar bone. Place your other hand on your belly button (do not massage with this hand). Switch both hands and repeat for about 30 seconds.

HOW TO DO THE STORY'S MOVEMENTS

The following pages are an explanation of the movements in this book, and their expected benefits.

Each page has a movement activity and a follow up question designed to promote an aspect of a child's development.

The author offers ideas and variations to each page, in the hope that the reader will adapt the movements and questions to offer choices and change to their children's movement experience.

A list of materials that enhance the story is also included.

As the teacher: You demonstrate the correct movement, leaving the children free to express themselves. All children are at varying ages and stages of development, so it is important to encourage them to do what they can; do not pressure children to do an activity that they are not developmentally capable of doing; adapt the story!

Page 54-55 Listening ears: This has several purposes. It takes attention away from play and other activities while getting the child to focus and listen. This method is used in kinesiology and acupressure to help with short-term memory, listening skills and language skills.

Page 56-57 Two-foot hop: This movement helps the child become more aware of both sides of the body; use both sides of the body at the same time; and develops postural control and whole body coordination.

Page 58-59 Balance tree: This movement helps the child develop an awareness of both sides of the body, gravity, space, balance, sequential movement, use of both brain hemispheres and development of the vestibular system.

Page 60-61 The laughing rocks: This helps the child with balance, stress reduction and a feeling of happiness and joy

Page 62-63 Crawling tunnel: This movement is a basic developmental stage which has a bilateral movement (the opposite arm and leg work together). This leads to being able to use both sides of the brain together, and will provide physical skills to help the child learn how to read and write.

Page 64-65 Whole body jump: May help with equal use of the whole body, balance, and being able to lift the whole body vertically off the ground.

Page 66-67 One-foot hop: Hopping helps to gain postural control of the whole body, and awareness of the shift in gravity as the child moves.

Page 68-69 Smelling Flowers : A resting activity involving aromatherapy, to calm and relax.

Page 70-71 Growing flowers: The movement teaches the child how to use tension and release to gain body control and relax. In Chi Kung it is used to energize the mind and body.

Page 72-73 Spinning wind: Spinning is said to improve children's learning abilities by moving fluid inside the inner ear, thus improving coordination and the vestibular system.

Page 74-75 Mountain hug: Hugging is said to provide a sense of companionship and happiness, reduce stress, and improve the quality of life.

Page 76-77 Balance ball: Balancing is said to develop learning through the vestibular and sensory systems. Throwing is said to develop a bigger brain.

Page 78-79 Balance catch: Balancing and catching develop hand/eye and physical coordination skills. Working with a partner develops teamwork, self-direction and social skills.

Page 80-81: Gorilla talk: Massaging the kidney 27s pressure points is said to increase energy levels, relaxes the body and helps both sides of the brain work together.

Note: All benefits listed in this book are from benefits to the author and observation of benefits to children in the author's care.
The movements are adaptations from various movement modalities such as Yoga, Martial Arts, Kinesiology, Chi Kung etc.

TEACHING TIPS

This page offers suggestions for using the story to enhance the child's learning experience, by allowing each child the freedom to explore each creative movement, according to his or her own stage of development.

As the teacher: Use puppets to begin and end the story. While reading the story, demonstrate each movement while being involved in the activity and process as it develops. Allow each child to be creative, observing the child's movements and adjusting the level of difficulty to suit the child. End the story by giving the child an animal stamp. Give praise and above all have fun!

Toddlers: Generally, are unsure of where they are in space; want to keep their feet safely on the ground; are learning to control their bodies; are afraid of gravity; and can generally only use one side of the brain at a time. With this group, use a flat piece of non-slip material (a rubberized painter's drop cloth works well, when you draw the elements of the story on it; (see "Materials" page 86). Lead the children through the story showing the story picture and demonstrating the movement. As the children become more adept in their movements introduce higher objects which will then lift them off the ground (e.g. the fallen tree as a balance beam which is a piece of 1x6 wood sanded smooth). Offer assistance by holding the child's hand lightly to steady the child while allowing them to learn by doing it themselves.

Listening ears: The ears are massaged from top to bottom with thumb and pointer finger. This may stimulate up to 400 acupuncture points in the ear. Younger children will not have the fine motor skills to do this movement but will attempt it.

Two-foot hop: This activity leads to a one-foot hop. The child uses imagination to become Gordy the gorilla. You hop from one foot to the other with arms down at both sides while making gorilla noises.

Balance tree: This is a balance beam. You walk across it by placing one foot in front of the other, heel to toe; (see "Materials" page 86).

The laughing rocks: Place the laughing rocks in various patterns and distances apart depending on the child's level of development. Use felt faces for toddlers and "Flip Flop Faces" for older children; (see "Materials" page 86)
As you step on the rocks laugh. Instruct the children to do the same.

Crawling tunnel: For toddlers hold the tunnel steady and give lots of encouragement. Keep the child in sight; (see "Materials" page 86).

Whole body jump: Both arms and knees swing up together, as you raise your feet off the ground and move forward. The child jumps over the balance tree; (see "Materials" page 86)

One-foot hop: Generally, toddlers will not be able to hop on one foot. To assist them have them hold onto the back of a chair and jump on one foot. Three to five year olds will be able to hop 3 to 10 hops respectively; try hopscotch games.

Smelling Flowers: Add a few drops of essential oil to some cotton balls or felt flowers and have the children guess the smell. Try to use smells that you have a picture of such as oranges, strawberries etc; which can be used to help the child get to know the smell.

Growing flowers: Use a watering can to sprinkle imaginary water on the children as they reach and push their roots (feet) into the ground.

Spinning wind: You spin both ways three times with your arms outstretched. For older children use a rotational balance board (two circular boards with a bearing between them that can spin as the child sits on it). Ask the child to be the wind. **SAFETY TIP:** Some children with brain dysfunction may be prone to seizures and should not spin or be spun around.

Mountain hug: With this activity ask the children to find someone to hug, or they can hug Gordy the puppet, or you.

Balance ball: With this activity use a ball or beanbag and Discovery Toys' basketball play center; use an ice cream pail; (see "Materials" page 86). Demonstrate and then let the children decide when they want to do it.

Balance catch: Toddlers find it difficult to catch a moving object. To create successes stand close to them and drop the beanbag in their hands. Give lots of praise; e.g. "Great job! You caught it". A balloon can also be used to slow things down; explain the balloon can burst and be aware of choking hazards.

Gorilla talk: Demonstrate this movement by placing the thumb on one side of the neck and fingers on the other side. Move the fingers down until you hit the collar bone, jump over it and massage the soft spots between the collarbone and the first set of ribs. Place the opposite hand on the navel; do not massage with this hand; make gorilla noises.

MATERIALS TO ENHANCE THE STORY

Story puppets: The story character, Gordy the gorilla, can be made in the form of a hand or finger puppet.

Animal stamps: Animal stamps can be bought at dollar stores.

Story telling cloth: A 5 foot x 12 foot painter's drop cloth sheet with the story drawn on the sheet; ideal for toddlers (See page 88).

Balance tree: Make from a 1x6 for toddlers and a 2x4 for older children, sand it smooth, draw on the tree with felt markers, and lacquer. The leaves are cut from artificial green grass. The river in the story can be cut from an old shower curtain and attached to the wood with pins.

Laughing rocks: For toddlers cut 6" circles from felt and draw happy faces on them with a marker. Use an iron on backing material to create a non-slip surface. For older children use "Flip Flop Faces" (a beanbag game from Discovery Toys).

Crawling tunnel: Can be bought from Ikea, or Toys-R Us; cardboard boxes can be put end to end; or a table with a blanket over it.

Smelling flowers: Dollar store flowers can be set in a block of Styrofoam or use cotton balls; add a drop of essential oil of a smell of your choice.

Growing flowers: Use a plastic watering can or large can or pail.

Spinning wind: Rotational balance boards (two circular boards with a bearing between them that can spin as the child sits on it).

Balance ball: Use small soft balls, or beanbags from dollar stores.

Balance catch: Use larger balls, balloons, Koosh balls or bean bags from Toys-R-Us, or most toy stores.

Note; Small objects can be choking hazards for pre-school children.

Gordy visits The Mountains
the story mat

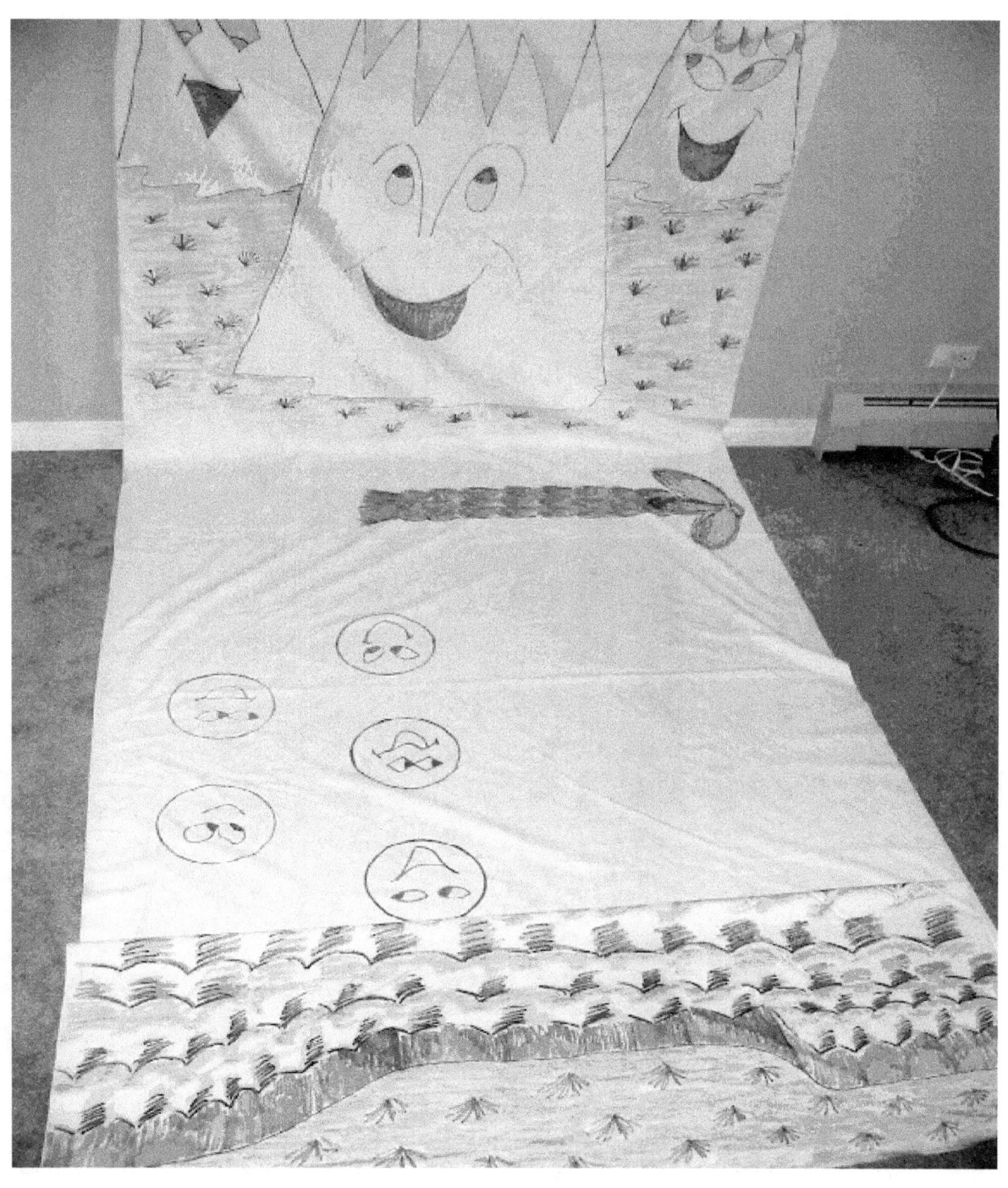

GORDY VISITS THE MOUNTAINS STORY MAT

"How to make the story mat"

The Story Mat follows the storybook "Gordy Visits The Mountains" available from: **http://www.lulu.com/spotlight/paulmackie**

The story mat can be made from any heavy material.
I use a non-slip (painter's drop cloth) rubberized cotton type material.
The size of the sheet can vary, depending on the floor space you have available.
The sheet you see in the pictures is 13 foot long by 4 foot wide and works well in most rooms.

Story sheet layout

mountains	tree	laughing rocks	river
4 foot long	2 foot long	4 foot long	3 foot long

4 foot wide x 13 foot long

The River

The river can be drawn on the sheet using colored felt tip pens.
This is what it should look like:

I use a piece of "swimming fish" plastic shower curtain that fits in the river; this looks like fish in the river.

GORDY VISITS THE MOUNTAINS - Story Mat

Crossing the River:
A piece of 1x6x48 inch fir can be used as a palm tree.

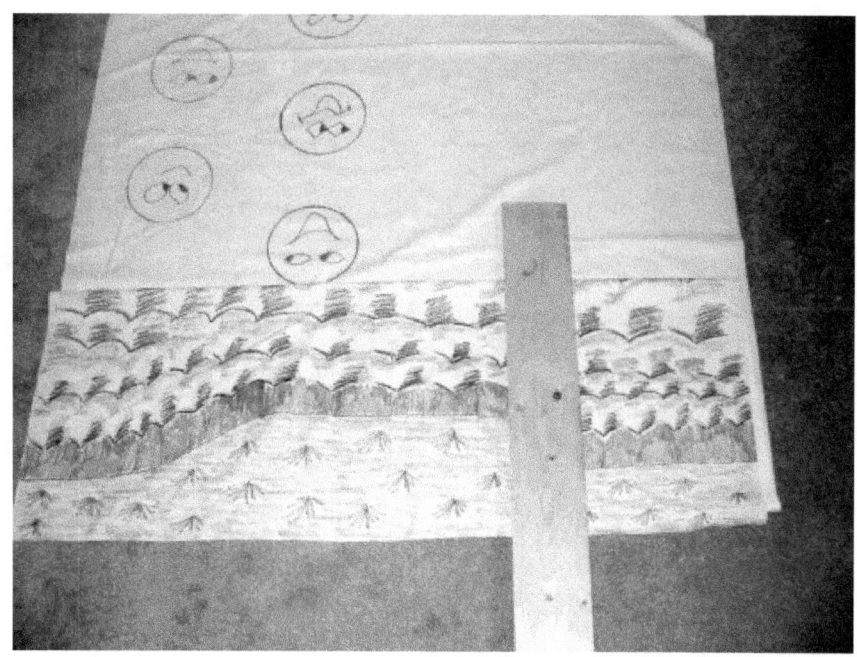

The tree can be drawn on the sheet

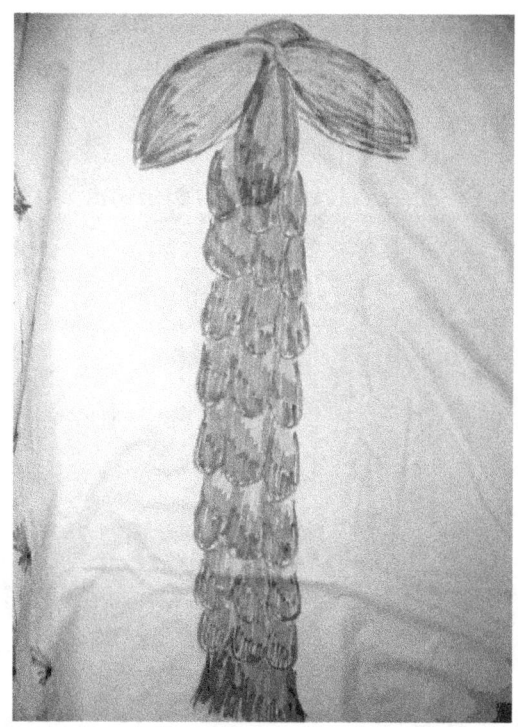

The tree can also be drawn on the wood, and some grass matting can be used for the leaves.

GORDY VISITS THE MOUNTAINS - Story Mat

The Laughing Rocks:
The rocks can be drawn on the sheet.

The laughing rocks can be bought as half circle, plastic flip flop faces from Discovery toys, cut from 6 inch felt, or cut from 1x6 fir with the faces drawn on the wood.

Some rocks can have different expressions and there are 6 faces in all.

GORDY VISITS THE MOUNTAINS - Story Mat

Balancing Tree:

This is the same tree as the one crossing the river. The tree can be made of wood or drawn on the mat.

The Mountains:
The mountains are drawn on the mat.

GORDY VISITS THE MOUNTAINS - Story Mat

Materials to enhance the story

Story puppets: The story character Gordy the gorilla can be made in the form of a hand or finger puppet.

Animal stamps: Animal stamps can be bought at dollar stores.

Story telling cloth: A 5 foot x 12 foot painter's drop cloth sheet with the story drawn on the sheet (ideal for toddlers).

Balance tree: Make from a 1x6 for toddlers and a 2x4 for older children, sand it smooth, draw on the tree with felt markers, and lacquer.
The leaves are cut from artificial green grass. The river in the story can be cut from an old shower curtain and attached to the wood with pins.

Laughing rocks: For toddlers cut 6" circles from felt and draw happy faces on them with a marker. Use an iron on backing material to create a non-slip surface.

For older children use "Flip Flop Faces" (a beanbag game from Discovery Toys).

GORDY VISITS THE MOUNTAINS - Story Mat

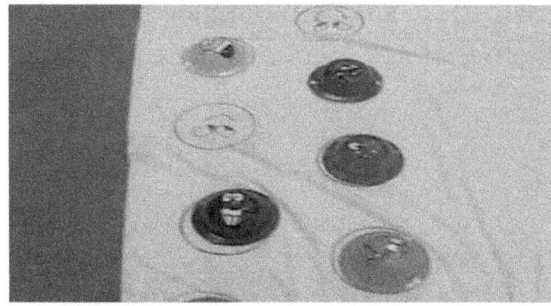

Crawling tunnel: Can be bought from Ikea or Toys-R Us. Cardboard boxes can be put end to end.

Smelling flowers: Dollar store flowers can be set in a block of Styrofoam, or use cotton balls.
Add a drop of essential oil of a smell of your choice.

Growing flowers: Use a plastic watering can or large can or pail.

GORDY VISITS THE MOUNTAINS - Story Mat

Spinning wind: Rotational balance boards (two circular boards with a bearing between them that can spin as the child sits on it)

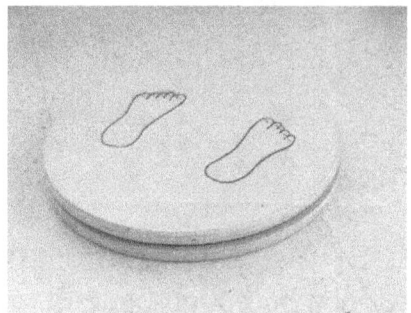

Balance ball: Use small soft balls or beanbags from dollar stores.

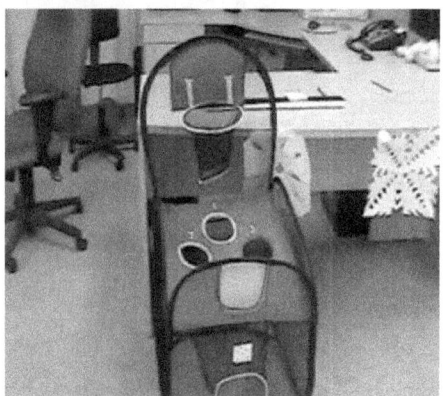

Balance catch: Use larger balls, balloons, Koosh balls, or bean bags from Toys " R "Us, or most toy stores.

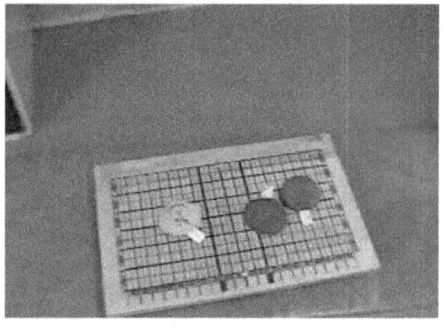

MOVING TO RELAX

Over the years I have looked for self-development techniques to meet my needs and reduce stress.

I found many techniques that I have used to help me reduce stress, and improve my thinking and communication skills; I have adapted some of those techniques and put them together in the form of Moving To Relax.

I have used the techniques with children, special needs children and adults; and myself for 20 years. Through anecdotal observation, I have noticed various benefits for myself and those who I have taught; my claims are based on those observations.

SOME POSSIBILITIES

☺ Increased self-esteem.
☺ Increased self-control.
☺ Calms and relaxes children and adults.
☺ creates a calm and relaxed environment
☺ Overcome learning stress.
☺ Make changes in routine easier.
☺ helps children be more self directing
☺ Empower parents and teachers to make a difference in their children's growth.

My general feeling is that the practitioner of the techniques will at least get some enjoyment, and a sense of wellbeing from the movements.

These movements are part of the "Educational Child's Play" stories and activities", which were designed to give children and adults, meaningful day activities and enhance learning abilities. The activities in this section are presented in adult form, so you can present them to children in the correct way; the same movements are in the storybook "A Walk in the Jungle", but in storybook form for children.

This section explains how to do each movement and gives a visual, printable page picture, to help guide you, when presenting the activity to others.

Each activity is placed on its own individual page, please feel free to copy and post the pages as part of your lesson plan; all other copyright restrictions apply.

Consistency is the key, when presenting the movements; as the teacher, you always present the correct movement. Children will try to copy the movement but may not have enough fine motor skills to do the exact movement.

FRIENDLY WAVE

May help with: Listening, balance and memory.

Why it is important: Developing the ability to listen, retain information and have whole body co-ordination are essential skills for easy learning and good social interaction.

How it is done: Tilt your head, placing your ear on the Shoulder, while extending your arm forward. With your hand draw an infinity sign (an 8 on its side) the width of your shoulders, focusing your eyes beyond the finger tips. Your body and arm move as one unit with no twisting at the hips. Do several times with each arm.

LISTENING EARS

May help with: Listening and focusing skills.

Why it is important: Attention is taken away from other activities while getting participants to focus and listen.

How it is done: Grasp each ear with the thumb on the inside rim and the pointer finger on the outside rim. Uncurl the ear down to the ear lobe using the pointer finger along with the thumb. Bring pointer finger and thumb back to the top of the ear and repeat several times.

WATER

May help with: Learning and energy levels.

Why it is important: Water helps conduct the electrical and chemical processes of the brain for clear thinking.

How it is done: Having a water bottle close by is an easy way to take a drink during the story.

ENERGY BOOST

May help with: Increased energy and relaxation.

Why it is important: Being relaxed and energetic makes learning easier.

How it is done: Place your hand on your neck (palm on the Adam's apple) with thumb on one side and fingers on the other. Move your hand down until you feel your collar-bone, jump over it and massage the soft spots between the next set of ribs and the collarbone.
Place your other hand on your belly button (do not massage with this hand). Switch both hands and repeat for about 30 seconds.

CROSSOVERS

May help with: Accessing the whole brain.

Why it is important: Using both sides of the brain is essential, for reading, comprehension and body coordination.

How it is done: Lift your left leg and touch your left knee with your right hand. Put the foot down and lift your right leg and touch your right knee with your left hand. Repeat, three or more times.
Participants having difficulty can match colored bands or stickers placed on opposite hands and knees.

CONNECTIONS

May help with: De-stressing and easier learning.

Why it is important: Being relaxed and focused helps make learning easier and improves self-esteem.

How it is done: Ask the participants to stand, or lie on the floor, cross their feet at the ankles and give themselves a big hug by placing their hands under each arm pit; can be done sitting or lying down.

BACK ARCH

May help with: Improved posture, concentration and tension release.

Why it is important: After sitting for long periods, slightly arching the back helps release body tension, improve posture and concentration.

How it is done: Resting on your elbows, lie face down on the floor and slightly arch your back by lifting your head backwards. Relax by bringing your head down. Repeat several times.

MASSAGE YAWN

May help with: Energy and verbal expression.

Why it is important: Having more energy, a relaxed jaw and facial muscles make it easier for participants to think clearly, communicate, or sing. The roaring sound helps participants express themselves.

How it is done: Put your fingers on your cheeks. Find the pivotal points of the jaw by opening and closing the jaw. While yawning, massage the points with the fingers. A yawning or roaring sound can be made.

TENSION AND RELEASE

May help with: Relaxation and body control.

Why it is important: The movement teaches how to use tension and release to gain body control and relax.

How it is done: Reach straight up as high as you can. Spread your fingers wide and push your feet down to the ground. Push and reach together; this puts the body into tension. Sway from one foot to the other; this can release tension; repeat several times.

VISUALIZATION

May help with: Visualization and problem solving.

Why it is important: Being able to picture what is going on in the mind's eye is an important skill in problem solving.

How it is done: Close your eyes and imagine the sun as various colors, shapes and sizes, ask about feelings; remember, there are no wrong answers.

The Balance Board

AN EXCEPTIONAL PIECE OF EQUIPMENT THAT MAY HELP CHILDREN AND ADULTS DEVELOP THEIR FULL POTENTIAL

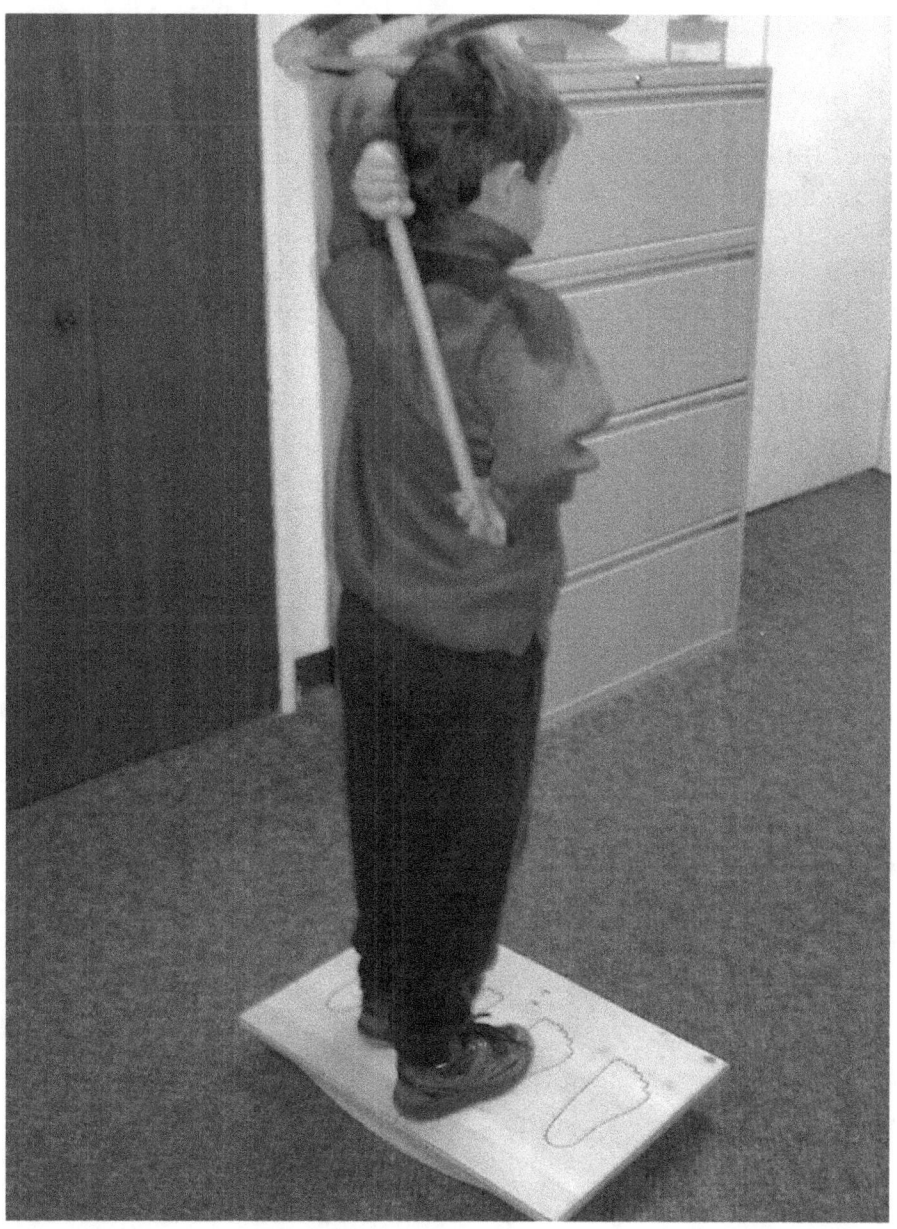

The Balance Board
It is my belief that the Balance Board is an exceptional piece of equipment, that may help children and adults develop their full potential.

THE BALANCE BOARD

Some care must be exercised when using the Balance Board, especially if the user is prone to seizures or has poor body coordination.

Some concerns are:
- Spinning can cause seizures, especially those that have sensory difficulties.
- Getting on and off the Balance Board can be difficult for some people, usually due to the sudden movement of the board.
- Always consult a doctor, or sensory therapist If you observe sensory difficulties (seeks or avoids sensory stimulation, poor coordination, unsure of body position in space, easily distracted, not able to focus, unusual behavior, etc.).

I have used Balance Board activities with:
- babies, by holding them in a sitting position on the board.
- pre-school children, as part of my storybook activity.
- with school children and college students studying for tests.
- special needs adults and the elderly; they all seemed to enjoy the activities.

I personally use the board daily to help center and focus myself before the day starts.

The activities can be printed and placed on the wall as a reminder of what to do.

I cannot guarantee results by practicing these activities. The benefits listed are purely anecdotal, based on observed benefits to myself and others in my care.
I suggest you try them. It is my hope that they work for you, as they did for me.

THINGS WE CAN DO ON THE BALANCE BOARD

The Rotational Balance Board
This Balance Board Is generally used to help develop spatial awareness (where you and objects are in space), and vestibular difficulties (the vestibular system controls movement and balance).

SAFETY: The Balance Board should always be set-up on a non-slip surface.

we can lie and spin

we can sit or kneel

we can stand and spin

BALANCE BOARD ACTIVITIES

Pass the Koosh Ball

Pass the stick

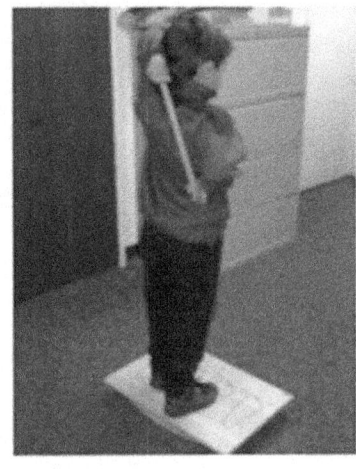

Read a book

Study for a test

Eyes closed

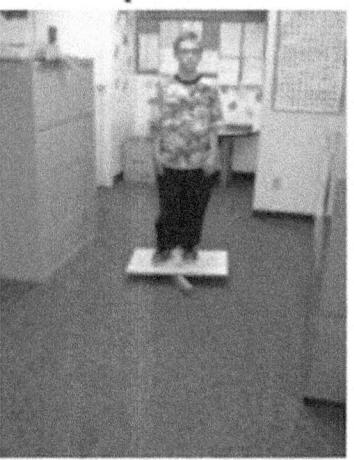

Pass ball to partner

PASS THE STICK OVER YOUR SHOULDER

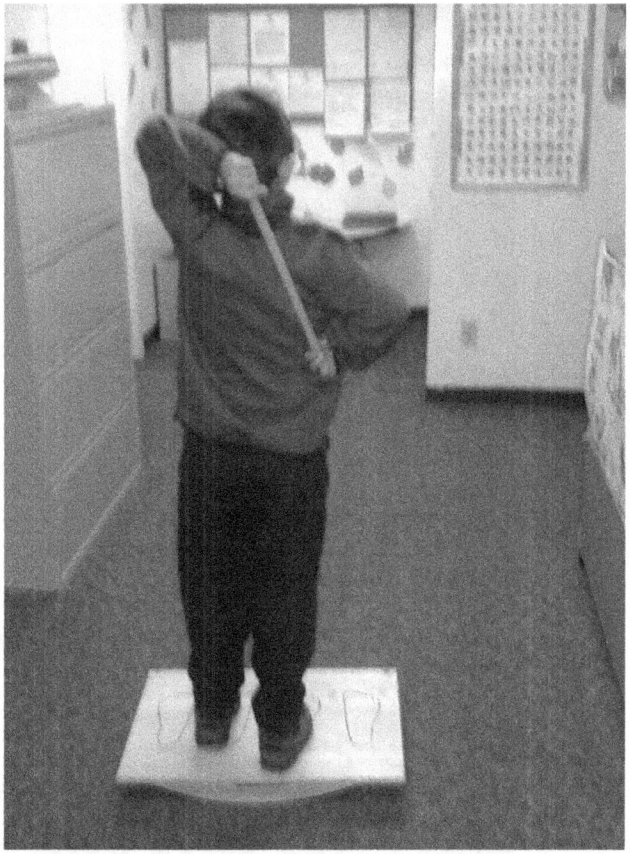

Pass the stick over left shoulder, then right shoulder.

Count out loud the number of passes in 1 minute.

Possible benefits:
          coordination and concentration.
          being able to figure out difficult tasks.
          number sequencing.
          increase in memory.
          awareness of where things are in space.

THROW KOOSH BALL AT A TARGET

Stand on board and throw koosh ball at the target.

Adjust board's level of difficulty.

Throw two koosh balls, one with left hand then one with right hand.

Possible benefits:
        hand /eye coordination.
        timing and sequencing abilities.

THE ADJUSTABLE BALANCE BOARD

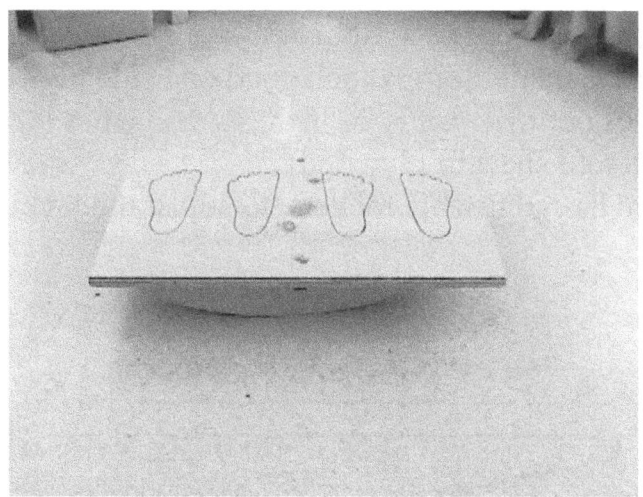

The Balance Board should be placed on a non-slip surface.

This board can be used to activate the vestibular system; which may help with easier learning of information, focusing the mind and balancing the body.

This Balance Board can be adjusted to easy, or difficult by rotating the semi-circular rockers under the board.

Adjust the board as children become more adept and familiar with it.

Caution: I recommend that you always consult a doctor before you attempt any Balance Board exercise.

HOW TO MAKE THE BALANCE BOARD

The Adjustable Balance Board:
The board Is made from ¾ inch good one side plywood.
The boards optimal size is 24 inches x 16 inches (you will get 11 from a 4 foot x 8 foot sheet of plywood).
The board has adjustable rockers, to adjust the level of difficulty.

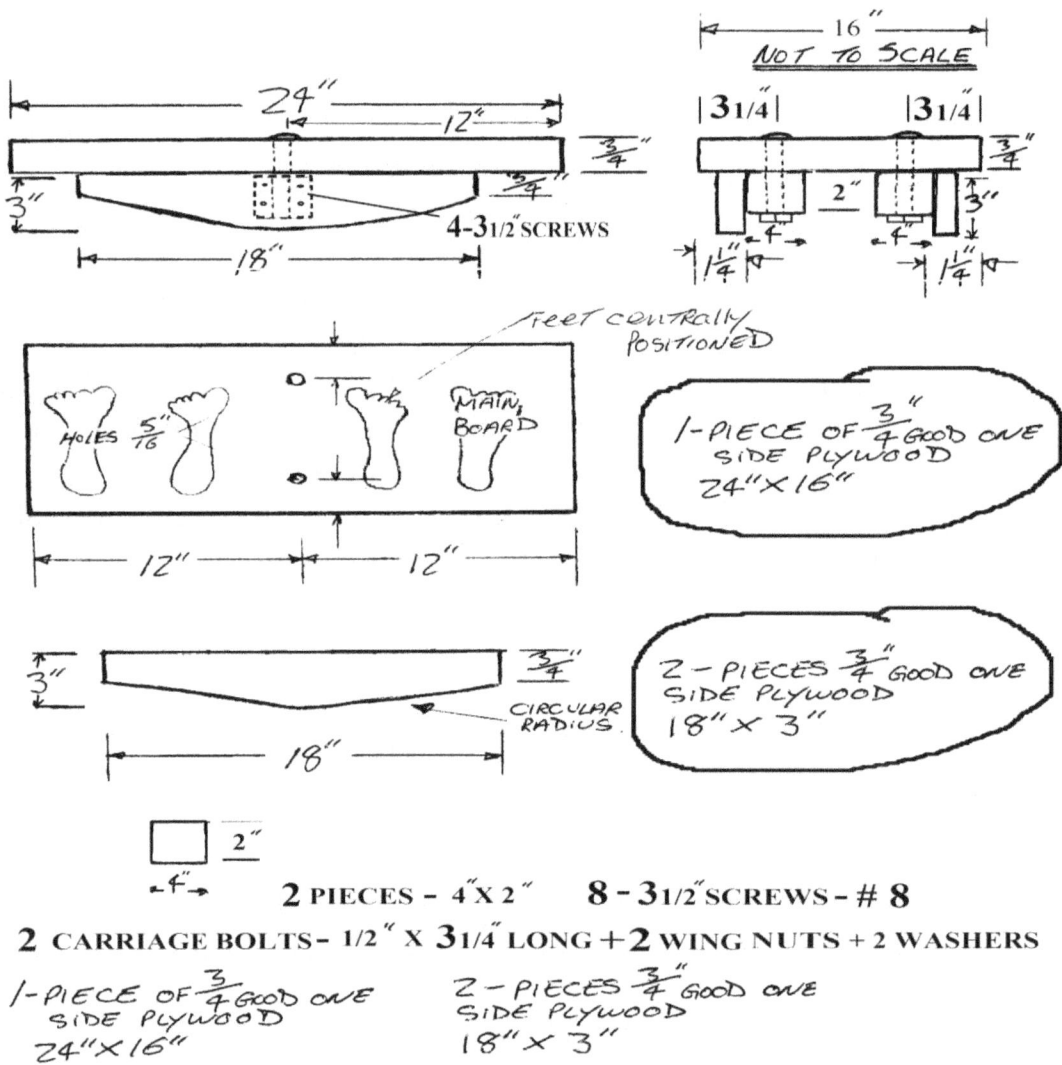

The Passing Stick

Made from a 1/2 inch piece of round dowling, 24 inch or 12 inches (if you have more flexibility), rounded off at both ends.

HOW TO MAKE THE ROTATIONAL BALANCE BOARD

The Rotational Balance Board:
- The board Is made from 2 pieces of ¾ inch good one side plywood.
- The boards optimal size is 16 inches in diameter. You will get 9 boards (18 pieces) from a 4 foot x 8 foot sheet of plywood.
- A 12 inch Lazy Susan (rotational cupboard bearing) bearing is placed centrally between two pieces of plywood.

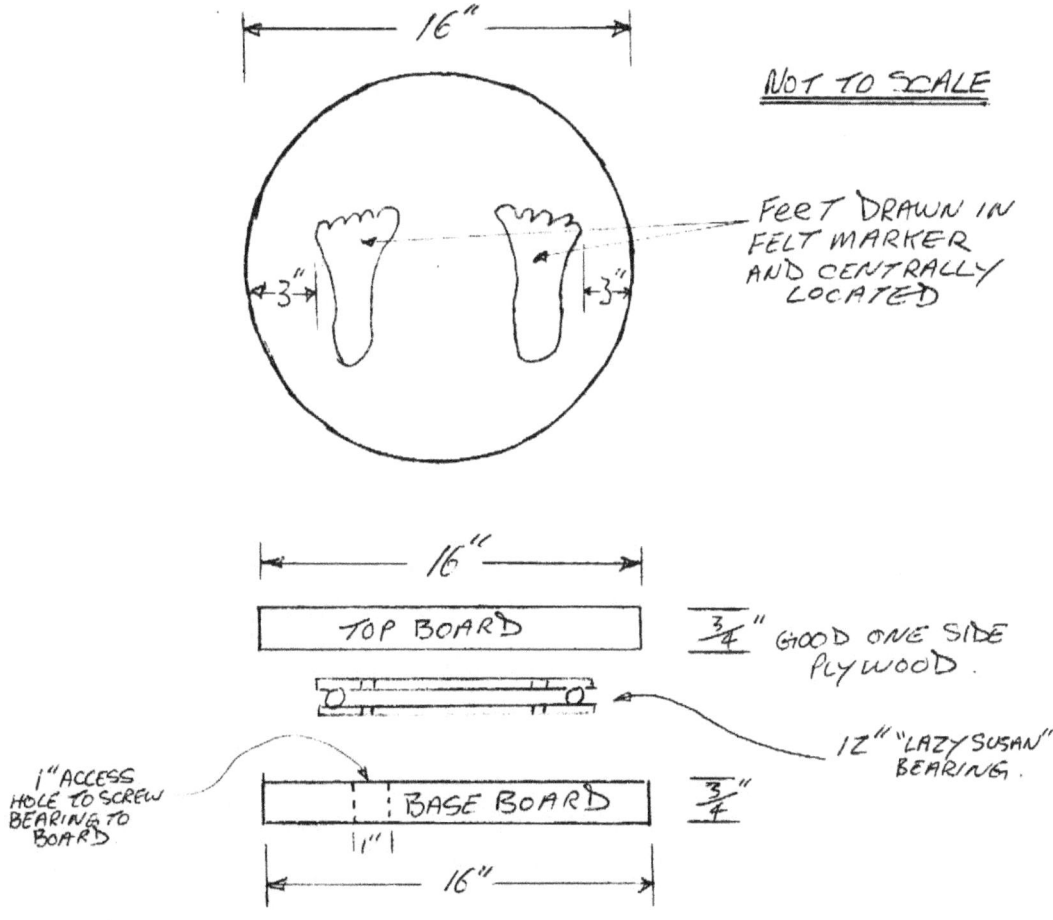

The board can be clear laquered and have a sprinkling of sand applied, to give a non slip surface to the board.

Materials needed:
   2 pieces of 16" diameter good one side plywood.
   1 "Lazy Susan" bearing
   Some screws for the bearing mount.

THE SENSORY ENVIRONMENT

Sensory carts are mobile activity centers, giving children choices.

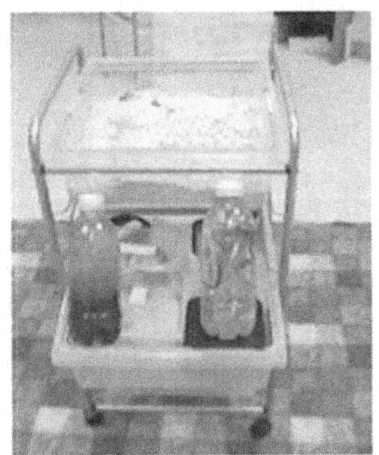

This Sensory Activity Cart is made from a mobile storage unit. It stores some of the sensory activity projects listed in this book.

In this picture you can see some sensory bottles in the lower drawer along with some textured pieces of material for a visual and tactile experience.

In the top drawer are some oats with different objects to provide a tactile activity.

Sensory Sand Table

This Sensory Sand Table was made from a two shelf cart.

Added to the lower shelf were some storage drawers which store different containers and sand play equipment.

The sand pit on the top shelf is the lower half of a plastic water table.

Mobile Activity Center

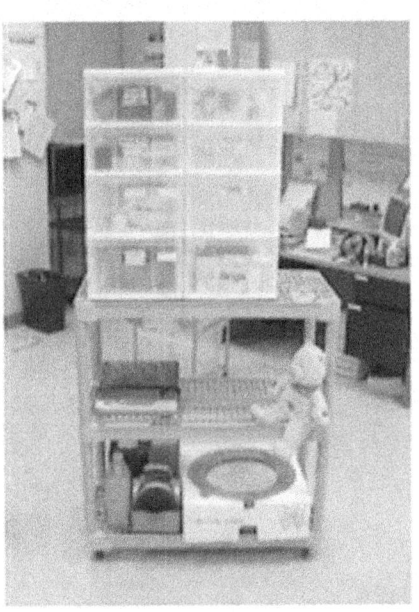

This cart is made from a three shelf cart.

It has storage drawers on the top shelf which store games, magazines, books, crafts, puzzles, grooming bags (nail clippers, hair brush, scissors etc), musical instruments, tapes/CDs, dried flowers and scented potpourri, and other any other activities suitable for the participants age group.

The lower two shelves hold larger items such as soft toys, sensory lights, tape/CD player and other sensory equipment.

The Sensory Environment

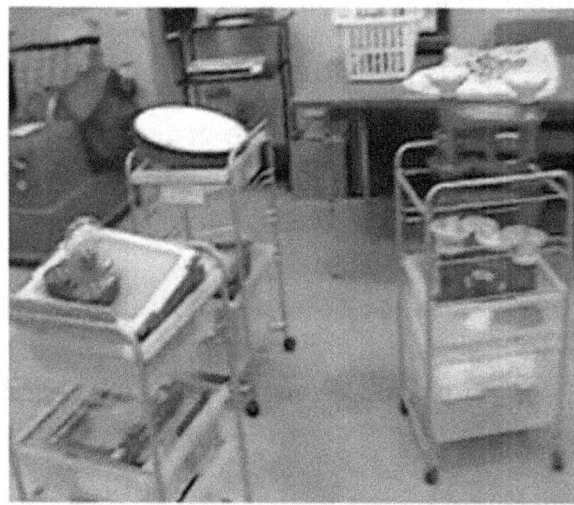

Sensory carts can be theme, sensory, or play based.
These examples show a music cart, a toy play cart and a visual/tactile cart.

Sensory carts can be set up to develop 7 senses. Sight; Sound; Touch; Hearing; Smell; Proprioception- body awareness of its position in space.
Vestibular-balance and the effects of gravity.

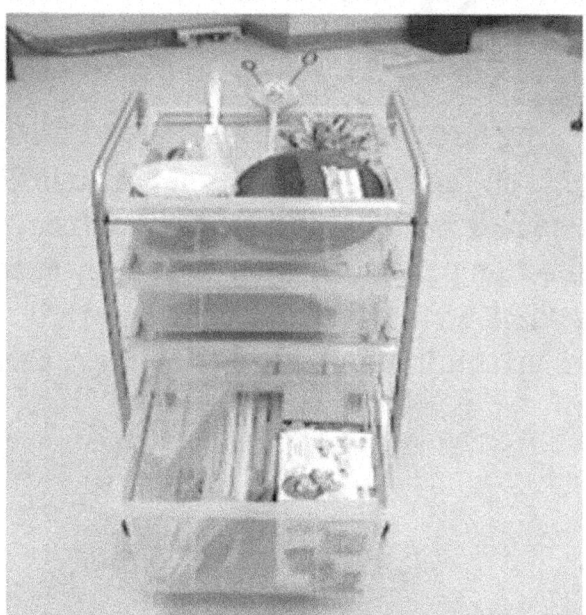

Sensory carts can be for all ages and have fun activities that stimulate the senses.
Sensory carts for the elderly can have nostalgic photographs and memorabilia, to stimulate the memory and enhance socialization.

Lights, aroma therapy, visual and tactile activities can be placed on the cart.
Always remember, safety first; all items should be age appropriate.
Choking and seizures tend to be the most common dangers.

Light Carts

Light carts can be made from larger 3 or 4 shelf units.
Any type of light can be used, they should be colorful, or have an unusual lighting effect.
It is a good idea not to use strobe lights, as they tend to create seizures in some people. I have used Christmas lighting, especially the type that flash off and on in a timed sequence.

Safety is important from an electrical perspective and do not wrap string lights around participants (choking hazard and heat from lamps can burn). The wiring for the light carts can be done by attaching power bars at the back of the unit and running all wires along the frame, or at the back, so they cannot be seen.
Fluorescent curtains or decoration can be added to the cart, with a black light shining on them for effect.

This light cart has square patterned Christmas lights on the side, various types of lamps, spinning disco balls with lights reflected off them, mirrored reflection panel, black lights, fluorescent material curtains, strip lights and some decorative monkeys to help children to relax during the experience.

The room is usually darkened for the light cart. When first using the cart, only turn on one or two lights at a time, as some children can be overwhelmed by the excessive visual stimulation.
Always observe the children for any adverse effects.

Sensory Activity Walls

This sensory wall was created by first scanning a picture into a computer and turning that picture into an overhead projection sheet.

The projection sheet was then placed on an overhead projector and the photographic image projected onto a wall.

The image was traced and painted onto the wall.

Lattice fencing and craft store flowers were added at the bottom of the painting to give a 3 dimensional effect.

If you look closely at this picture you will see another real picture (in the middle slightly to the right) of a sidewalk cafe.

The wall painting is an extension of the original and gives the impression of a 3D walk in cafe.

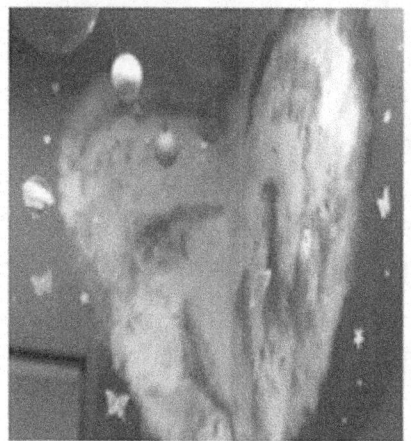

This effect is created by projecting light through colored discs onto the wall and ceiling.

The room itself is painted black, has a planet mobile, black lights, fluorescent stars and reflective stickers on the wall.

The planets and colored lights revolve around slowly to give a very relaxing sensory experience.

Sensory Activity Walls

This sensory wall is made with interactive cogs and gearing that can be rotated.

On either side of the large wheel are interactive puzzles and activities like a child's play center (bells, beads, things that turn etc).

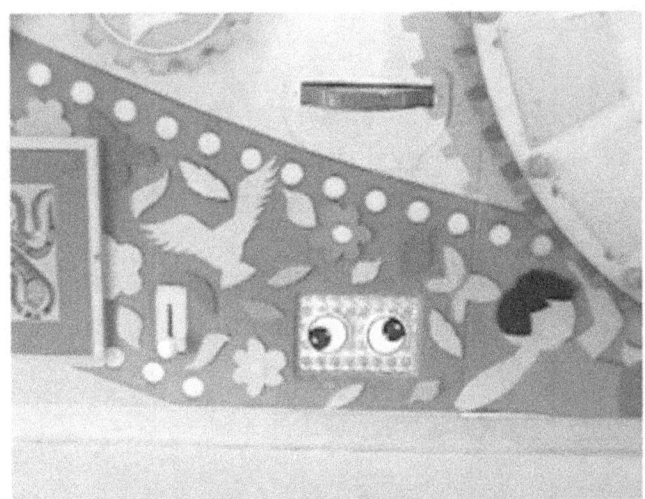

This wall is a closer view of the first picture.

It has levers, interactive games and things to push and turn.

The wall itself is very colorful and the pictures are inviting.

This wall has the picture of a train painted on it.

In front of the wall picture is an interactive control panel.

To the left and right (not in picture) of the control panel are seats and small doll-house-sized station buildings.

SENSORY ENVIRONMENTS WHY? WHAT? WHERE? AND HOW TO DO IT?

WHY?
Sensory environments can be therapeutic or just plain fun!
My feeling is to proceed with caution when presenting sensory environments to someone who may have a sensory problem. Those problems can range from seizures, behaviors, defensiveness, etc. I only mention this to make you aware that there could be problems that need professional advice.

My intent is to provide an environment that may reduce behaviors, provide meaningful day activities, and above all be fun for the children.

WHAT?
Sensory rooms are generally of two types: a dark (black), or a light (white) room. They can range from inexpensive up to $40 thousand dollars, depending on what you want to have in the room.
In my experience, the dark room can be created for about $500.
I will explain how to set up a dark room. A white room can vary greatly, so I will direct you to more professional sources for equipment and installation.

Also included in this book are other types of sensory environments, and some of the equipment you can provide to make it more appealing.

WHERE?
Sensory rooms can be built just about anywhere; my personal recommendation is to make it as big as possible, but not less than 6 foot square; even a closet would work.

HOW TO DO IT?
Depending on your intent, and the age of children who will use the room, there will be several ways to interact. Generally, you would let the children explore the room, without much guidance, or interaction from you.
In most cases you monitor the children for any adverse reactions, such as, behaviors, under, or over stimulation, medical problems, seizures etc.
If the children ask you to participate, then you would; otherwise, just observe.

When using the portable sensory environments, you would set up the environment and interact, until the children are engaged in an activity, then disengage, so they can explore; use your discretion.

The whole idea of the sensory environment is for free exploration, choice making, cognitive growth and a fun activity for children.

CREATING A DARK PLANET ROOM

When creating the sensory room, it is best to have a theme; the easiest to get items for, is a planet, or space room.

Flaghouse and maybe some local stores stock sensory lights, revolving planets and other neat sensory items. I have also found sensory items in flea markets, Wal - Mart, light fixture stores and garage sales; just keep your eyes open.

Dark rooms are usually black, so paint the interior of the room flat black, this includes all surfaces of the room; any white areas will show when you install the black lights.
I left a circular area in one corner of the room (about 3 foot diameter) white, so the projected image would have a nicer effect.

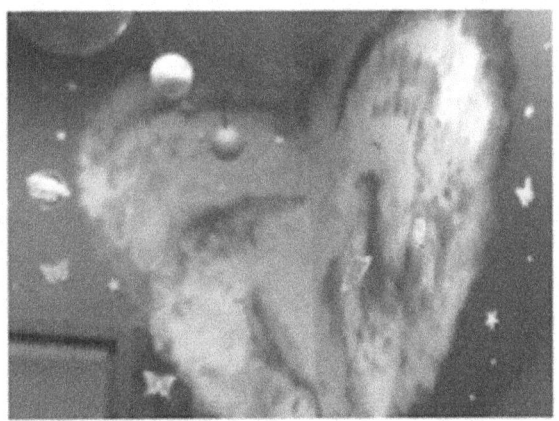

Leave a 3 foot white area for the projector image.

Install two 24 inch black lights, on opposite walls (at the top), or on the ceiling. The black lights (which usually have their own switch built in) can be plugged into an outlet, or if possible switched separate to the lighting system.
Make sure you get a qualified electrician to do any re-wiring to the existing electrical system.

In my installation there were two electrical outlets, wired to a switch that was separate to the existing lights, which were left, as is.

The room I created was for special needs adults, so I had the plug outlets located at the top of the wall near the ceiling and located all the equipment as high as possible in the room.

Install the rotating planet system. This is about 5 foot in diameter and needs to be in the center of the ceiling.

CREATING A DARK PLANET ROOM

revolving planet, black light and wall hanging

Install the projector in the opposite corner to where you have the white unpainted circle.

To mount the projector, I bought a corner shelf and mounted it as close to the ceiling as I could; the projector beam is adjustable and has a varying focus to sharpen the projected image. The projector comes with several oil filled circular discs that rotate and create a moving image on the wall.

The projector will need to be below the revolving planets, so that the projected image is not blocked by the planets.

Locate the stars and planets evenly around the walls and on the ceiling.

Hang the planet material on the walls under the black lights. I got the planet material from Wal Mart and painted it with dollar store fluorescent paint.

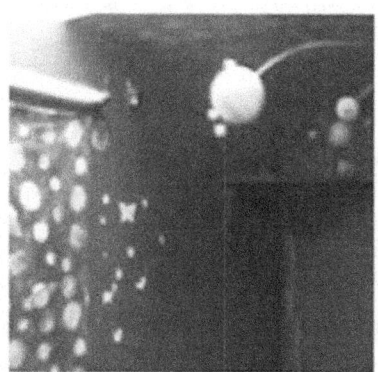 

Fluorescent materials are placed under the black lights, stars and planets are stuck on the walls and ceiling.

Mount the CD player on a corner shelf. The CD player I bought had a remote, which causes fewer disturbances; once you are using the room.

CREATING A DARK PLANET ROOM

Music and lighting effects add to the sensory experience.

The black room can also have various types of lights; I have found Christmas lights that hang like a curtain, to be most effective.

Place the bean bag chairs in the room and you are ready to experience the sensory planet room.

One other thing that can make the space room quite unique is the "Flaghouse Vibro Music Cushion". The cushion is expensive at about $1700, but the sensory vibration and auditory sound of a rocket ship taking off in a visual slideshow is truly an amazing experience; for all ages.

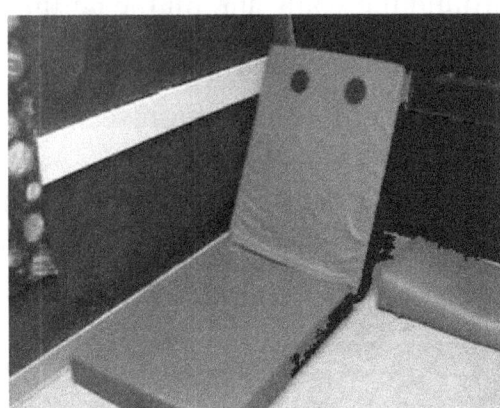

Flaghouse Vibro Music Cushion and wedge

The white room is similar in construction but requires everything to be white. Visit Flaghouse for their catalogue and some great sensory ideas: http://www.flaghouse.com/SnoezelenAL.asp

CREATING A DARK PLANET ROOM

Step by step in pictures:

paint room black, add stars and planets

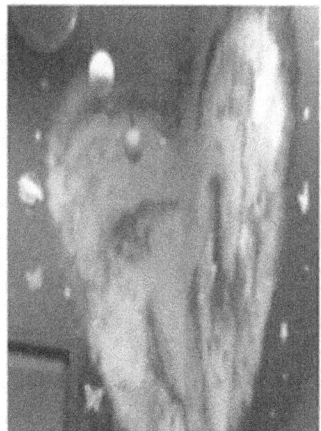
leave a 3 foot area white

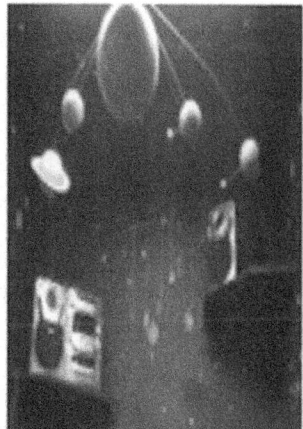
mount the planets and stereo system

mount 2 black lights and fluorescent material under them

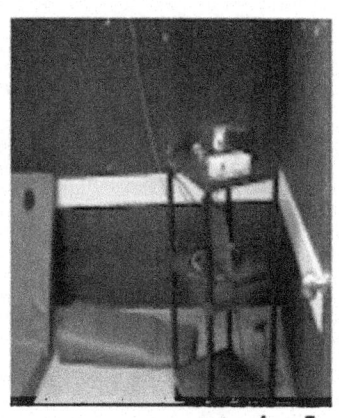
use a computerized projector, or a projector mounted on a wall shelf

add bean bag, close the door and enjoy

Cost to make room:

Black paint……………..$20, 2 black lights……………..$60
Revolving planet……….$80, Projector………………....$80
Luminous stars…………$20, Luminous planets………..$20
CD cassette player……..$80, Bean bag chairs………....$80
Corner shelves…………$50, Planet material………......$10

Total cost……………approx: $500

SENSORY ENVIRONMENTS VESTIBULAR ACTIVITIES

Vestibular activities are related to balance and the effects of gravity (quick movement activities can be alerting while slow movement activities can be calming).

Watch children closely during these activities and only present them when the children are physically able to do them.

Spinning:

scooter board   park merry-go-round   swivel chair

Note: spinning can cause seizures in some children.

Swinging:

wheelchair swing   tire swing   garden swing

swing slowly

VESTIBULAR ACTIVITIES

Walking on different surfaces:

grass to concrete   grass to woodchips   large stepping rocks

Note: always check for sharp objects if in bare feet

Walking on different surfaces:

pea gravel   colored tennis court   large gravel and rocks

PROPRIOCEPTIVE ACTIVITIES

Proprioception is an awareness of the body in relationship to its position in space. Proprioceptive activities can have calming effects on the nervous system.

Pushing and Pulling:

 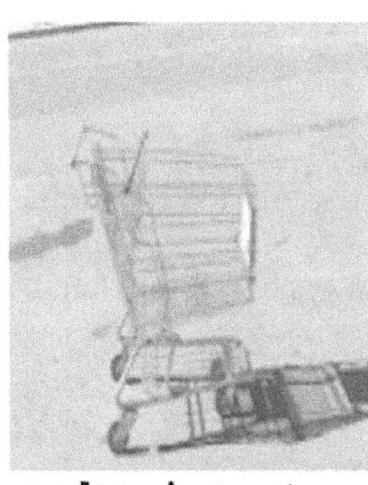 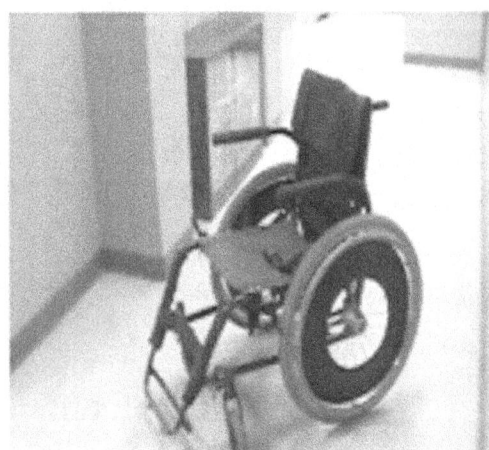

vacuum cleaner　　　shopping cart　　　wheelchair

 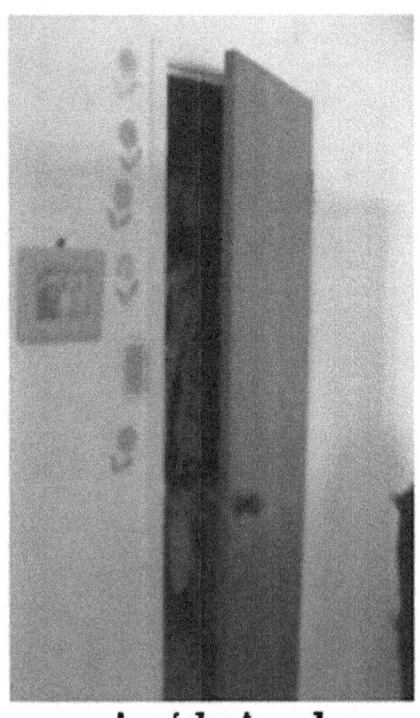

pushing on walls　　　opening/closing doors

PROPRIOCEPTIVE ACTIVITIES

Hanging by Arms:

parallel bars

monkey bars

Carrying Heavy Loads:

laundry basket

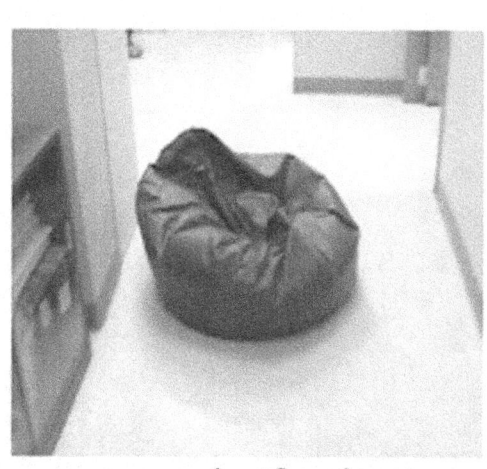
moving furniture

Exercising:

climbing stairs

swimming

Visual Sensory Activities

According to Carla Hannaford, Ph.D., in her book "Smart Moves", the eyes gather sensory images necessary for learning. The brain uses these images along with other sensory information to create a visual perception system.

Vision Activity Bottles

BUBBLY BOTTLE

water
one -1 litre clear plastic pop bottle
food coloring (different colors)
liquid dishwashing detergent
tape (electrician or duct tape)
glue (plastic, contact cement or crazy glue)

1. half fill the bottle with water
2. add half a cup of detergent
3. add food coloring
4. tighten cap and tape or glue shut

SHAKE FOR BUBBLY FUN

GLITTERY SNOW BOTTLE

water
one -1 litre clear plastic pop bottle
colored glitter, tape, glue

1. put a cup of colored glitter in the bottle
2. fill to the top with water
3. tighten cap and tape/glue

SHAKE FOR GLITTERY FUN

Vision Activity Bottles

COLOURED CONFETTI BOTTLE

water
one -1 litre clear plastic pop bottle
colored (plastic) confetti shapes
tape, glue

1. put a cup of colored confetti in the bottle
2. fill to the top with water
3. tighten cap and tape/glue

SHAKE FOR COLORFUL FUN

DESERT ANIMAL BOTTLE

one -1 litre clear plastic pop bottle
small toy desert animals
yellow play sand, tape, glue

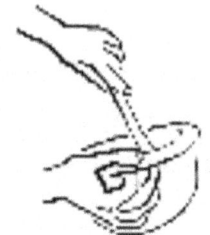

1. fill the bottle half full with play sand
2. add desert animals
3. tighten cap and tape/glue

SHAKE AND TURN

Vision Activity Bottles

FISHY SEA BOTTLE

water
one -1 litre clear plastic pop bottle
blue food coloring
toy sea creatures, seashells, tape, glue

1. put toy sea creatures and seashells in the bottle
2. add water nearly to the top of the bottle
3. add a few drops of food coloring – fill water
4. tighten cap and tape/glue

SHAKE AND TURN

BALL BOTTLE

one -1 litre clear plastic pop bottle
cooking or low grade motor oil
various weights, sizes of balls and marbles, tape, glue

1. put in the marbles and balls
2. fill nearly to the top with cooking or motor oil
3. tighten cap and tape/glue

TURN UPSIDE-DOWN AND OBSERVE

Vision Activity Bottles

LETTER MEMORY BOTTLE

small plastic letters
one -1 litre clear plastic pop bottle
sand or salt
tape

1. half fill the bottle with sand or salt
2. add about 10 plastic letters
3. tighten cap and tape

SHAKE THE BOTTLE WHAT LETTERS DO YOU SEE? SHAKE AGAIN DO YOU SEE ANY WORDS? SHAKE AGAIN WHAT DO YOU SEE?

NUMBER MEMORY BOTTLE

one -1 litre clear plastic pop bottle
10-15 different plastic objects
sand or salt
tape

1. half fill the bottle with sand or salt
2. add about 10 – 15 plastic objects and tape cap

**SHAKE THE BOTTLE, HOW MANY OBJECTS ARE IN THE BOTTLE?
SHAKE UNTIL YOU ARE SURE.**

Tactile (Touch) Sensory Activities

According to Carla Hannaford, Ph.D., in her book "Smart Moves", the act of being touched stimulates sensory-motor growth and produces hormones within the brain that help with nerve net development.

Tactile Activity Bottles

MAGNETIC WAND

one -1 litre clear plastic pop bottle
plastic magnetic bingo chips
plastic magnetic bingo wand
water, tape, glue, string

1. fill the bottle about ¾ full with water
2. add about 10 or 20 small bingo chips
3. tighten cap and tape/glue
4. tie the string to the wand and tie the string to the bottle top

SEE HOW MANY CHIPS YOU CAN PICK UP

MIXING DOUGH

plastic measuring bowls, cups, spoons, knives, cookie cutters, flat tray, or bowl, and rolling pins
1 bag of flour, water, salt

1. put half the flour into the bowl, or tray, add in some water and a little salt
2. hit, mix, pound, squeeze until the dough is formed
3. cut, scoop, shape, roll and make impressions

BE CREATIVE

Tactile Activities

MULTI-COLOURED RICE OR NOODLES

regular dry white rice or noodles in bulk, Ziploc bags, food coloring or liquid Tempura paint (various colors), water. buckets, spoons, plastic cups, plastic bottles any containers you like

1. put a different color paint with rice or noodles in each Ziploc and mix contents by squeezing bags
2. put bag contents on a flat tray and when dry (or a low heat oven) put the rice or noodles in the sensory table with some containers

EXPLORE ADD WATER OR HAIR GEL LATER TO EXTEND THE ACTIVITY

BUBBLE BATH

water
dishwashing liquid, berry baskets, toilet paper tubes, bubble wands, straws, bowls, eggbeaters and anything that will blow a bubble.

1. fill bowls with water.
2. add lots of dishwashing liquid
3. add bubble maker items

**EXPERIMENT WITH WAYS TO MAKE BUBBLES
EXTEND ACTIVITY (DROP FOOD COLORING INTO WATER)**

Tactile Activities

MELTING CORNSTARCH

water
large bag of cornstarch
food coloring

1. put the cornstarch in the flat tray
2. mix enough water to make a paste
3. add food coloring

SQUISH AND SQUEEZE - WATCH IT DRY THEN BECOME LIQUID AGAIN

SNOW PAINTING

snow
water
several small containers and flat tray
food coloring (several colors)

1. put some snow in the flat tray
2. mix several containers of colored water
3. place the containers near the tray

START FINGER PAINTING THE SNOW

Tactile Activities

INDOOR GARDEN

one piece of grass sod
water
spray bottle
plastic scissors and flat tray

1. put a roll of grass sod in the flat tray
2. fill spray bottles with water
3. spray grass and let it grow

CUT GRASS WITH PLASTIC SCISSORS

PEANUT CHUNKS (STYROFOAM)

packing peanuts (Styrofoam packing)
water, large chunks of Styrofoam
spray bottles

1. put packing peanuts in the sensory table
2. add in some chunks of Styrofoam (from packing in boxes)
3. mix some water with some food coloring and fill the spray bottles

SPRAY AND RE-SHAPE THE PEANUTS

Auditory (Hearing) Sensory Activities

The work of Dr. Alfred Tomatis suggests that sounds can make the body's muscles react and are important to the learning process.

Auditory Activity Bottles

INDOOR RAIN BOTTLES

one -1 litre clear plastic pop bottle
one box of toothpicks, a bag of uncooked rice
small ¾ inch plastic discs
tape/glue

1. put the toothpicks in the bottle
2. half fill the bottle with uncooked rice
3. put 30 plastic discs in the bottle
4. tighten cap and tape/glue

SLOWLY TURN THE BOTTLE TO HEAR THE RAIN

RHYTHM BOTTLES

six -1 litre clear plastic pop bottles
sand, kidney beans, a drum
tape/glue

1. leave 2 bottles empty
2. put 4 inches of sand in two bottles
3. put 4 inches of beans in two bottles
4. tighten caps and tape/glue

HIT THE DRUM WITH THE BOTTLES LISTEN TO THE SOUNDS.

COUNT OUT DIFFERENT BEATS USING THE DIFFERENT BOTTLES.

Auditory Activity Bottles

DRUMMING BEANS

kidney beans, peas, lentils, rice
two or more drums, plastic containers
a piece of cloth or towel

1. place the towel or cloth in the bottom of the table (for the hearing sensitive)
2. put the two drums in the sensory table

POUR THE BEANS ONTO THE DRUMS (ADD THE PEAS, LENTILS AND RICE SEPARATELY)

MUSICAL MARACAS

water, strips of paper, tape, 8 pop cans
flour, paint, large beans, peas
small beans, small rocks

1. put beans, rocks or peas in the cans
2. seal lid with some tape
3. soak the paper strips in flour and water paste-cover cans with several layers of paper strips
4. when dry decorate by painting

SHAKE MARACAS

Auditory Sensory Activities

DRUM MAKING

margarine containers, large cereal boxes
large coffee cans, wooden doweling, wooden spoons,
cloth strips, tape

1. tape the lids on the cereal boxes, margarine containers and coffee cans
2. wrap some cloth strips onto the wooden doweling and wrap with tape

TRY DIFFERENT DRUM SOUNDS

SHAKER PLATES

small sized paper plates, small pebbles
large dry macaroni, small buttons
tape, staples

1. put a quantity of pebbles between two plates and staple them together
2. tape (over the staples) the plates
3. do the same for the macaroni and small buttons

EXPERIMENT WITH THE DIFFERENT SOUNDS

Auditory Activities

FINGER CYMBOLS

large and small jar lids
large bottle caps
elastic bands
hole-punch/scissors

1. match two bottle caps or jar lids
2. poke two holes in each cap or lid
3. feed an elastic band through the two holes and tie
4. put a cap or lid on thumb and forefinger of both hands

CLACK AWAY

Olfactory (smell)

Sensory

Activities

The work of Michael Leon, Ph.D. shows a link between learning, memory and smell activities.

Sensory Smell Activities

VEGETABLE DIP

8 -35mm dark film canisters
cotton balls
onion, turnip, cabbage, cauliflower, potato, peppers, cucumber, radish

1. poke a small hole in the top of each film canister
2. place a piece of each vegetable in each canister
3. put a cotton ball in each canister

GUESS THE SMELL OF EACH VEGETABLE

VEGETABLE MATCH

8 -35mm film canisters
cotton balls
onion, turnip, cabbage, cauliflower, potato, peppers, cucumber, radish
pictures of each vegetable

1. poke a small hole in the top of each film canister
2. place a piece of each vegetable in each canister
3. put a cotton ball in each canister

MATCH THE SMELL OF EACH VEGETABLE WITH THE PICTURE

Sensory Smell Activities

FRUIT COCKTAIL

8 -35mm film canisters, or containers
cotton balls
orange, lemon, strawberry, melon, grape, mango, banana, peach

1. poke a small hole in the top of each film canister
2. place a piece of each fruit in each canister
3. put a cotton ball in each canister

GUESS THE SMELL OF EACH FRUIT

FRUIT MATCH

8 - 35mm film canisters
cotton balls
orange, lemon, strawberry, melon, grape, mango, banana, peach
pictures of each fruit

1. poke a small hole in the top of each film canister
2. place a piece of each fruit in each canister
3. put a cotton ball on top of fruit in each canister (the cotton ball hides the piece of fruit)

MATCH THE SMELL OF EACH FRUIT WITH THE PICTURE

Sensory Smell Activities

FLOWER POTPOURRI

flowers (go to the florist or supermarket and ask for any old flowers with different textures and smells)

1. remove the petals off the different flowers and put them in a flat tray

SORT THEM BY SMELL, COLOUR AND SIZE WHY ARE THEY DIFFERENT?

CLEAN DIRT

toilet roll
warm water
soft soap (perfumed type)
grater and flat tray

1. rip up the toilet roll into small pieces and put in the flat tray
2. grate some bars of perfumed soap and put that in the mix
3. add some warm water and mulch it all into a thick paste

EXPLORE THE TEXTURES AND SMELL

Sensory Smell Activities

SANDY COFFEE

ground coffee
cornmeal
vanilla and cinnamon extract
containers flat tray

1. mix equal parts of cornmeal and ground coffee in the flat tray
2. after a while add in the vanilla and cinnamon extracts

EXPLORE THE DIFFERENT SMELLS

COLOUR SMELL

water
yellow, red, green, golden brown food coloring
peppermint, lemon, vanilla and cinnamon food extracts
containers flat tray

1. half fill the flat tray with water
2. put in yellow food coloring and lemon food extract
3. explore patterns and colors
4. next time put in green/peppermint, golden brown vanilla, cinnamon/red

MIX AND EXPLORE THE SMELLS AND PATTERNS

Gustatory (taste) Sensory Activities

Our sense of taste gives the brain information about the things we eat, memory and our senses.

Sensory Taste Activities

TASTY DRINKS

straws
unsweetened grapefruit juice, apple juice
sweetened orange juice, Pepsi or Coca-cola
cups with lids you cannot see through

1. place a straw in each of the juices
2. put your finger over the end of the straw and remove it from the liquid
3. place the straw over your tongue and remove finger (letting juice fall onto tongue)

GUESS WHAT TYPE OF JUICE IT IS

SWEET AND SOUR

apples such as: McIntosh crab apples, Granny Smith, Golden Delicious, or Red Delicious
pictures of each apple paper plates or containers

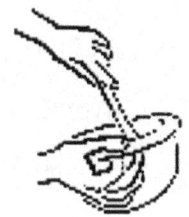

1. cut the apples into small pieces
2. place the pieces on a paper plate
3. eat an apple piece; match it to a picture;
4. describe how it tasted

WAS IT SWEET, BITTER OR SOUR?

Sensory Taste Activities

TASTING PLATES

4 paper plates
salt
sugar
vinegar
coffee

1. place a little salt, sugar, coffee and vinegar on four separate plates

TASTE EACH SUBSTANCE AND SEE WHETHER IT IS SALTY, SWEET, ACIDIC OR BITTER

POPCORN TASTING

popcorn, salt, sugar
vinegar
cheese

1. prepare some popcorn and divide it into four bowls
2. sprinkle some sugar on one bowl of popcorn, salt on another, cheese on another and vinegar on the last

TASTE EACH TYPE OF POPCORN IS IT SALTY, SWEET, ACIDIC OR BITTER?

FUN DAY ACTIVITIES INTRODUCTION

Fun Day activities can vary from child to child, what works for one child may not work for another. It is not my intent to explain, define or say that certain activities will have a specific outcome; I suggest you find out for yourself what works and what does not.

Activities in Fun Day Activities have been chosen for children and adults, as possible activities to try; or ideas for discussion; or ideas to explore that may give a child a meaningful day. The ideas are from the author's own experiences and   research but may not necessarily be the author's own ideas.

Similar activities may appear in other publications; if an idea is copyrighted please contact the author and it will be removed. or recognition given.

Some activities, while listed in a certain category, may fit into other categories.

The following list of ideas can be explored and expanded upon.
Some ideas may be work related and not even produce a creative outcome, but they are there for you to explore with children.

Possible outcomes:

- Give meaning to life.
- Calming and relaxing.
- Increase awareness of what relaxation activities there are.
- Decrease anxiety.
- Expand creativity.
- Increase confidence and self-esteem.
- Increase focus and adaptability.

Finding a Fun Day activity for children can be a problem but doing so can lead to increasing a child's confidence, self-esteem, and give a child a knowledgeable meaningful day.

The following pages are practical activities for a wide range of ages and personal preferences and hopefully you will find something that suits you.

Some activity ideas are general in nature; and there is blank space on each page to write your own ideas. Bubble diagrams is a way to expand on or brainstorm an idea.

BUBBLE DIAGRAMS.

As I mentioned above, "Some ideas are general in nature", so I have included the Bubble Diagrams section to help you brainstorm the ideas.

With bubble diagrams, we brainstorm ideas and quickly jot down our thoughts as they flow.

A good way to start this process is to start with a central theme, then make a single bubble for each idea that comes to mind (keep the bubble text that comes off the main theme to one or two words).

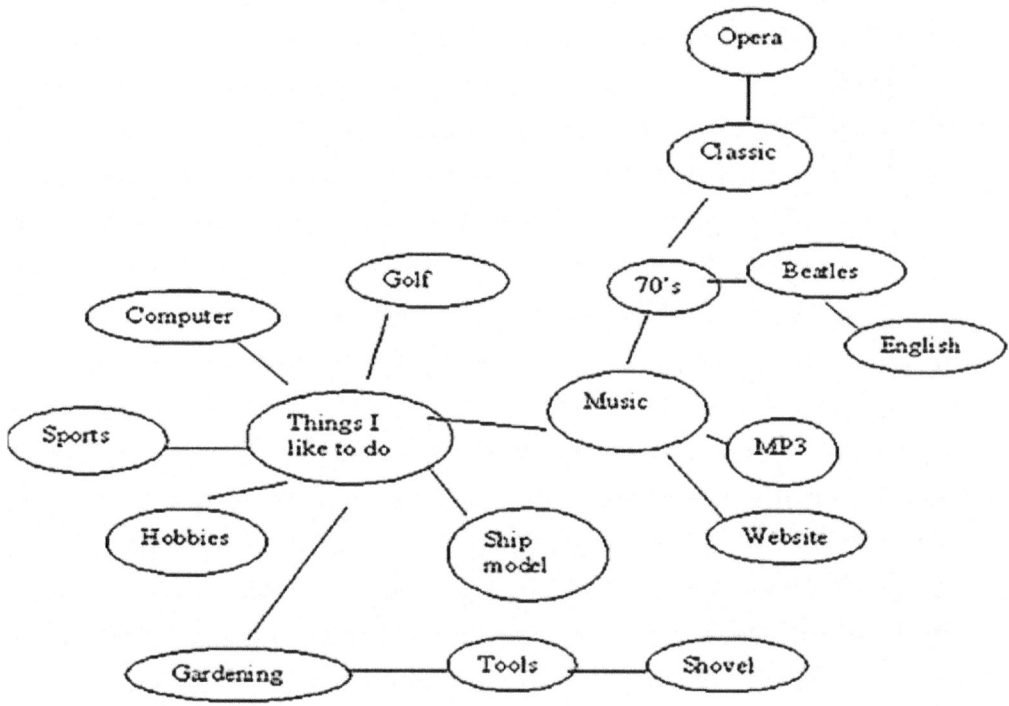

Don't focus on one idea, just write the thoughts down as quickly as possible.

Once you have a series of thought bubbles it is time to expand on each thought bubble, until you have several topics that may interest you.

If one of the thought bubbles was "hobbies" you would then list all your thoughts on hobbies: golf; swimming; sewing; knitting; woodworking; car repair; stamp collecting.

Then take each thought idea and expand on that: Golf - where-when-with whom-clubs-equipment; Swimming - where-when-what type; Sewing - what-machine-tapestry-needle point, etc.

BOOKS

Reading books
Comic books
Short storybooks
Writing a book
Book club
Autobiographies
Recycling books
Book fair
Biographies
Visit Library
Magazines
Book of stamps
Used book exchanges
Book repair
Inspirational books
Book videos
Making book markers
Books on tape
Car book
Braille books
Reading to others
Illustrating books
Job in book store
Publishing industry
Internet book club
Collect phone books
Sports book
Entertainment book
Cook book
Coloring book
Book review
Make a book case
Book publishing
Coupon book
Baby book
Memories book
Bookmobile

BOWLING

Glow bowling
Critique different bowling alleys
Disco bowling
Have bowling parties
League bowling
Lawn bowling
Bowling fund raiser
Make bowling shoes
5 pin bowling
Bowling clothes
Lawn bowling
Bowling lawn care
Bowling art
Bowling tips
Bowling magazine
Bowling trophies
Bowling instructor
Set up a competition
Run the snack bar
10 pin bowling
Assist in a bowling alley
Online bowling
Write bowling ball review
Bowling pro shop
Repair bowling equipment

CITY TRANSIT

Transit bus
Visit bus station
Handi bus ride
Visit bus machine shop
Journey on bus
Visit body shop
Bus manufacturer
Bus maintenance depot
Mechanic
Cleaner
Journey on Train
Visit train station
Train driver
Bus driver
Visit rail yard
Research buses
History of transit
History of trains
Transit schedules
Transit maps
Washing buses
Commuting
Motor coaches
Greyhound bus
Greyhound history
High speed rail
Park and ride
A cross country train ride

CARNIVAL RIDES

Go-carts
Handy-boat
Mall carnivals
Heritage Park
Calgary Stampede
Trip to Disneyland
Amusement arcade
White water rafting
Canada Olympic Park
Canoeing
West Edmonton Mall trip
Sky diving
Trail riding
Sailing
Special needs balloon rides
Ticket sales
Carnival history
Circus
Circus animal trainer
Carnival ride safety
Makeup artist
Animal trainer
Carnival artist
Carnival driver
Ride mechanic
Ride operator

CHILDREN

Boys and girls club
Summer parks
Summer camps
Teaching children
Child care at fitness center
Puppet theatre
Children's Festival
Between Friends clubs
Daycare worker
Big Brother/Sister
College child care
Kiddies Corral at fair
Lunchroom supervisor
School volunteer
Children's hospital worker
Children's clothes
Tell children's stories
Make children crafts
Child magazine
Child nutritionist
Make children's furniture
Make birthday cakes
Children's book club
Library storyteller

CHINESE CULTURE

Traditions
Religions
Chinatown various cities
New Year celebrations
Fortune cookies
Acupuncture
Kites
Herbal medicines
Fireworks
Martial arts
Cork art
Tai chi
Ping pong
Chi Quong
Medicine
Kung fu
Writing Chinese
Opera
Chinese movies
Languages
History
Food
Chinese tea
Chinese philosophy
Chinese astrology
History
Numerology

CLEANING

People's houses
Park maintenance
Pet service
Floors
Adopt a park
Bars
Wiping tables
Laundry
Churches
Cleaning person
Recycling
Basements
Car wash
Organizing
Offices
Windows
De-cob webbing
Graffiti
Janitorial duties
Carpets
Dry cleaning
Cleaning product sales
Spring cleaning
Septic tank cleaning
Deck cleaning
Roof cleaning
Commercial cleaning
Upholstery
Fish tank cleaning
Car cleaning
Vinyl siding
Cleaning silver/metals
Washing/laundry
Hotels/motels
Spring cleaning
Building maintenance
Cleaning service
Clean seniors residences

CLOWNING AROUND

Face painting
Jell-O bobbing
Mini Olympics
Bubble blowing
Food fight
Clown
Sidewalk painting
Races
Pizza store clown
Balloon animals
Karaoke
Magic tricks
Bad jokes
Dress up
Hot tub party
Doodling
Theatrical sports
Dancing
Team Mascot
Playing drums
Playground
Parties
Parades
History of clowns
Art clowning
Clowning skits
Street clown
Clowning improvisation
Clown clothes
Clown makeup artist
Teach clowning
Clowning course

COLORING

Crayons
Coloring pencils
Water color paints
Holiday coloring pages
Oil paints
Seasonal coloring pages
Flower coloring
Coloring books
Paint by numbers
Color collages
Melt crayons onto paper
Finger painting
Colored cardboard models
Face painting
Food coloring art
Mandala coloring
baking with food coloring
Doodling
Sketching
Color by number
Coloring occasion cards
Adult coloring pages
Coloring with chalk
Colored tissue paper

COMMUNITY

Seniors pals
Swimming
Park outings
Coffee group
Collecting rocks
Playground visits
C-train officer
Airport attendant
Hospital patient visits
Sign language class
Comedy club
Exercise work out
Multi-cultural group
English classes
Day care
Join Seniors Clubs
Biking
Shakespeare in the park
Community theatre
Tours at museum
Own a lunch truck
Tours at science center
Attend festivals
Fishing
Traveler
Visit community college
Community college courses
Course teacher
Community radio visit
Community television
Recreation centers

COMPUTERS

Make a website
MP3 music files
Write E-books
Educational games
Digital camera
Create games
Shopping EBay
Open Email account
Online auctions
Research interests
Marketing
Play games
Public domain research
Chat rooms
Computer repair
Create a chat room
Play Computer games
Computer sales
Program trainer
Computer security
Virus removal
Make computer furniture
Computer sciences
Distance education
Lap top repair
Make computer software
History of computers
Network installer
Computer animation

DANCING

Organize dance
Make costumes
Go to dance recitals
Teach dancing
Host a community dance
Interview dancers
Dancing lessons
Break dancing
Write a book on dance history
Square dancing
Choreography
Ballet
Watch dance movies
Ballroom
Acting and dancing
Form a dance club
Collect dance movies
Write a book on dance
Explore history of dance
Favorite dance music
Dance competitions
Styles and techniques
Evaluate various studios
Belly dancing
Salsa dancing
Break dancing
Make dance videos
Swing dancing
Dancing music
Irish dancing
Hip Hop dancing
Tap Dancing

DENTIST

- Dental hygiene
- Practice good oral hygiene
- Receptionist
- Make tooth paste
- Alternate oral care
- Create hygiene program
- Visit dental office
- Dental assistant
- Fix dental equipment
- Online Research
- Cosmetic dentist
- Family dentist
- Dentist jokes
- Holistic dentist
- Denture dentist
- Endodontist
- Periodontist
- Orthodontist
- Sedation
- Body and teeth research
- Chirodontics
- Braces

DRAWING

Sidewalk art
Colored paper art
Tattoo art
Painting
On walls
Art class
Chinese letters
On floor
Still life
Drawing with both hands
On ceiling
Animals
Nature art
On wood
Transportation
Water colors
Face painting
People
Oil painting
Hand painting
Charactures
Using charcoal
Leg painting
Cartoons
Colored pencils
Foot painting
Crayons
Nose painting
AutoCAD drawing
Technical drawing
Portraits
Drawing Faces
Drawing horses
3D drawing
Sketching
Animation
Tracing

FLOWERS

Grow flowers indoors
Grow flowers outside
City gardens
City parks
Flower Varieties
Flower boxes
Flower meanings
Library books on flowers
Potpourri
Party planner flowers
Knitting flowers
Drawing flowers
Flowers and countries
Flowers and herbs
Dried flowers
Flower arranging
Flower delivery
Flower collage
Sewing flower patterns
Flower encyclopedia
Flowers for weddings
Flower meanings
Flower months
Flower colors
Flower cultural meanings
Where flowers grow
Flower care

FOOD

Baking
Food bank
Mystery shopper
Breakfast for kids
Food critic
Nutritionist
Brown bag lunches
Food for thought
Own a restaurant
Cake decorator
Food preparation
Restaurant deliveries
Canned goods maker
Gourmet chef
Soup kitchens
Catering
Grocery shopper
Supplier for canteens
Concession stands
Hot dog stand owner
U pick farms
Cooking classes
Lunch programs
Vegetable garden
Dietician
Lunch truck
Waiter/waitress
Drop in centers
Meals on wheels
Weight watchers
Food chain
Food delivery
Food safety
Food preparation
Appetizers
Wines and beverages

HELPING OTHERS

Friend to seniors
Adopt a grandparent
SPCA
Housekeeping
Visiting at a nursing home
Hospital volunteer
Volunteering at a shelter
Food bank
Dog walking
Internet service
Assisting a friend
Library storyteller
Help seniors garden
Meals on wheels
Flower shop assistant
Recycling
Home visits/seniors
Salvation Army
Lemonade stand
School volunteer
Volunteer pet sitting
Reading stories to elderly
Cleaning up garbage
Repairing things

HORSES

Horseback riding
Farm
Horse shoeing
Rodeos
Watching parade
Circus
Riding stables
Horse drawn carriage
Ranching
Mounted police
Cattle driver
Rural vet clinic
Horse racing
Outrider
Jockey
Horse shows
Feeding horses
Pony rides
Horse breaking
Cleaning/caring for horses
Hay rides
Branding
Breeder
Horse owner
Horse photographer
Chuck wagon races
Trail riding
Selling horses
Horse tack
Carousel horses
Arabian horses
Dressage horses

JEWELRY

Collect photos antiques
Jewelry tattoos
Host jewelry show
Henna
Make and sell
Jewelry repair
Work in jewelry store
Appraiser
Open own store
Get a small ear stud
Watch repair person
Polishing stones
Jewelry cleaning person
Jewelry fundraiser
Jewelry museum
EBay – auction jewelry
Get piercing
Research jewelry stores
Jewelry boxes design
Jewelry boxes making
Bead jewelry
Jewelry design
Wooden jewelry
Anklet jewelry
Brooches
Pendants
Birthstones
Precious stones

LEADERSHIP AND YOUR LEGACY

Lead a music group
Self portrait
Organizing events
Traveling
Owning a business
Family trees/genealogy
Teaching a skill
Writing a book
Mural scrapbook
Video biography
Written biography
Crafts you make
Writing letters
Sidewalk art
Sculpting and selling work
Mentoring
Leadership forum
Leadership journal
Research women leaders
Spiritual leadership
Leadership magazine
Teamwork
Leadership qualities

LIBRARY

Write a best sellers list
Public domain books
Library assistant
Re-write old books
Working at a book store
Re-stock book shelves
Book review club
Repair books
Reading group
Story teller
Develop library for peers
Internet Research
Write a book
Reading magazines
Visit public library
Law library
University library
Library catalogue
Dewey decimal system
Electronic resources
Microfiche
Books in print
Mobile library

MONEY

Rolling coins
Money management
Investments
Fund raising
Accounting courses
CEO of a bank
Collecting foreign money
Spendthrift
Trader
Bartering
Budgeting
Stock market
Shopping
Computer programs
Collecting change
Casino
Count money
Lottery
Piggy bank
Coin rubbings
Set up bank account
GST tax
Bank teller
Taxes
Money conversion
Visit bank
Accounting
Money orders/cheques
Play money games
Counterfeit money
Credit cards
Loans
Government grants

MOVIES

Go to movies
Drive in movies
Movie reviewer
Movie actors
Wedding movies
Movie library
Work at community theatre
Movie trivia
Watch movies
Stunt person
Set-up movie night
Extra in a movie
Make a movie
Costume design
Watch DVD movies
Outdoor movies
Movie paraphernalia
War movies
Asian movies
Silent movies
Running a theatre
Makeup artist
Collect movies
Own a video store
Publicist
Movie critic
Star in a movie
Fund raiser/movie day
IMAX movies
Sell tickets
Write a screen play
Work at a movie theatre
Movie name game

MUSIC

Attend symphony
Music festivals
Work in a music store
Band critic
Orchestra
Make a CD on computer
Computer music MP3s
Organize a dance
Make a music video
Conductor
Play an instrument
Music appreciation group
DJ
Drumming
Research favorite music
Theme music
Music therapy
Music awards
Electronic music
Develop a CD
Radio station
Storytelling to music
Hand bell choir
Recording studio
Karaoke
Roadie
Lead a music group
Take music lessons
Make an instrument
Work at concerts
Write sheet music
Christian music
Music hall
Burlesque
Christmas music
Rock music
Music notes

NEEDLEWORK

Dress making
Macramé
Shoe binding
Quilt pillows
Tatting
Rug hooking
Silk ribbon embroidery
Sewing accessories
Cross stitch
Purse needlework
Petite point
Rug making
Tattooing
Wall murals
Braided rugs
Body piecing
Leather work
Tailoring
Needlework associations
Needlework frames
Needlework magazine
Catalogues
Needlework crafts
Wool needlework
Needlework websites
Used needlework books
Needlework machines
Sewing machines
Types of fabrics
Quilting
Felt patterns
Bedspreads
Knitting
Knitting patterns
Needlework patterns
Supplies

OUTDOORS

Summer hiking club
Eating outside
Parking lot cleaning
Camping
Barbeque
Dog walking
Tour guide
Brown bag lunch outdoors
Fishing
Bark collecting
Park maintenance
Horse riding
Tree study
Planting trees
Work at golf course
Rock collecting
Walking/running
Outdoor sports
Garden pond project
Yard work
Landscaping
Waterfalls
Door to door fundraising
Adopt a park
Wilderness walks
Rock sculptor
U pick farms
Barbeque
Work in sport goods store
Hiking
Cycling

PAINTING

Water color
Silhouettes
Folk art
Body paint
Canvas
Graphic design
Oil/charcoal/pastels
Have art show
Ceramics
Finger painting
Airbrushing
Flower pressing/painting
Murals
Painting cars
Stain glass painting
Research artists
Paint by numbers
Cartooning
Painting cards
Posters
Furniture painting
Pencil sketching
Draw the city
Caricatures
Shadow painting
Landscape painting
Stenciling
Tole painting
Sponge painting
Painting contractor
Fence painting
Room painting
Rock painting

PAPER SHREDDING

Secret documents
Packing material
Mobile shredding
Repair paper shredders
Shred paper
Teach others/supervise
Business/recycle
Paper making
Papier Mache
Craft collage
Piñata
Security service
Confetti maker
Industrial shredding
Office shredding
making crafts with paper

PARKS

Flower bed gardening
Clean a park
Walks
Adopt a park
Hill climbing
Walking pets
Water Park
Model airplane flying
Amusement park
Model ship sailing
Miniature golf
Train tours
Nature walks
Park tours
Park maintenance
Shakespeare in the park
Park games
Theatre shows in the park
Park play equipment
Visit theme parks
Parks and recreation
Hiking trails
Campsite surveyor
Skateboard Park
City playgrounds
Golf courses
Golf lessons
Ghost towns
Lakes
Farms
Rivers
Springs
Glaciers
Mountains
Waterfalls
Mountain biking
Music shows
Study wildlife

PEOPLE WATCHING

Attend a play/theatre
Wading pool
Public transport
Mall security
Indoor playgrounds
Airport greeter
Lunchtime supervisor
Wall Mart greeter
Visit a mall
Airport
Visit a park
Leisure centre
Arcades
Animal watching group
Musical performance
Folk festival
Visit a movie theatre
Visit the lake
Mall information person
Community theatre
Acting lessons
Community college

PIANO

Playing
Attending concerts
Organ
Writing music
Keyboard
Visit piano manufacturer
Research history
Tuning pianos
Bar/lounge acts
Types, jazz, classical,
Related instruments
Sound tracks
Restore pianos
Piano techniques
Concert master
Learn piano chords
Research music for piano
Make piano benches
Play
Play electronic piano
Piano songs
Blues piano
Christian piano
Piano dealer
Wurlitzer piano
Piano mover
Toy piano repair

PLANTS AND FLOWERS

Flower shop assistant
Indoor garden
Scrap booking
Sell flowers
Garden research
Visit nursery
Bar stroller
Terrarium
Help seniors garden
Flower supplier
Weeding
Farming
Grass cutting
Special gifts/occasions
Repotting plants
Start a greenhouse
Cuttings
Flower catalogue
U pick farms
Flower baskets
Bonsai tree growing
Valentines/mothers day
Flower garden
Hospital flowers
Growing new breeds
Card making
House plants
Desert plants
Cacti
Garden plants
Watering plants
Landscape plants
Growth of plants
Botany
Shrubs
Wetland plants

PRINTING

Chinese printing
Computer
History of printing
Pencil/pen/crayon
Potato printing
Braille
Alphabet
Screen printing
Foreign languages
Tee shirts
Paper/metal/wood
Novelty making
Wood burning
Cards
Tracing
Visit copy shop
Print business cards
Print wedding invitations
Local newspaper
Word puzzles
News letter
Window artist
Printing press
Government printing
Color printing
Label printing
CD label printing
Printing software
Scanning documents
Printing inks
Calendar printing
Printing envelopes
Used printing equipment
Design web pages
Visit local newspaper
Start your own paper

PUZZLES

Competition
Puzzle club
3-D puzzles
Framing puzzles
Recreational puzzle
Gift puzzles
Brain teasers
Puzzle party
Metal brain teaser puzzles
Murder mystery
Crosswords
Joke puzzles
Word puzzles
Strategy book/Internet
Wooden puzzles
Cryptic puzzles
Visit puzzle factory
Online jigsaw puzzles
Word search puzzles
Math puzzles
Make crossword puzzles
Sports crossword puzzles
Dot to dot puzzles
Fill it in puzzles
Riddles
Newspaper puzzles
Maze puzzle
Pogo
Arcade games
Conundrums
Anagrams

READING

Poetry reading
Learn speed reading
Research authors
Inspirational reading
Book reports
Book story tapes
Reading club
Book review
Journaling
Book exchange
Comics
Different languages
Book mobile
Magazines
Interpreter
Reading to elderly
Write a book
Book donations
Write an E-book
Reading marathon
Editing
Teaching to read
Computer reading programs
Reading comprehension
Palm reading
Reading strategies
Tarot card reading
Reading music
Proof reading
Phonics
Public domain books
Reading to children

RECYCLING

Pop can bottles
Research craft ideas
Auto wreckers
Newspapers
Creative art projects
Garbage person
Glass
Recycling exchange store
Land fill
Phone books
Garage sale
Furniture
Delivery
Gardening
Water recycling plant
Refill ink cartridges
Garbage removal
Composting
Magazines
Clothing consignment store
Baby and children's clothes
Recycling depot
EBay auction
Old jewelry to new
Computer parts
Car parts
Battery recycling
Cartridge recycling
Tire recycling
Recycling computers
Recycling containers
Composting
Building materials

RIDING IN VEHICLES

Safety awareness
Auto body repair
Amusement park ride
Bus
Airport tour
Submarine
Train
Plane maintenance tour
Helicopter
Ships
Handibus
Airport museum
Airplane
Car
Tank
Trucks
Bicycle
Military museum
Car wash
Naval museum
Auto body shop visit
Horse drawn carriage
Car manufacture plant
Garage visit
Double decker bus
Recreation vehicle visit
Bus depot visit
Rocket ship into space
Visit flight deck on an airplane
Visit heavy duty shop
Motor vehicle registry
Visit car dealerships
Collector vintage cars
Army vehicles
Electric cars
Golf cart

SCRAPBOOKING

Scrapbook store
Teach courses
Old cards
Wedding day
Taking pictures
Year book
Special occasions
Magazines
Relaxation therapy
Different design pages
Themes
Computer scrap booking
Memory sales rep
Creative memories
Photo essays
Stamp collector
Scrapbooking shows
Recycling scrapbooks
Baseball/hockey cards
Coin collecting
Reminiscing
Flower collecting
Collages
Old label collecting
Scrapbook poems
Scrapbook templates
Embossing
Rubber stamping
Scrapbook convention
Baby scrapbooking
Craft store
Scrapbooking hints
Punches for scrapbooking

SHOPPING

Personal
Make up counter
Grocery produce
Grocery
Shipping and receiving
Fish counter
Secret shopper
Flyer delivery
Butcher
Shelf stocker
Home delivery
Baker
Sales person
Courtesy clerk
Parking lot attendant
Gift shopping
Music shopping
Cashier
Sample demo person
Gift wrapper
Window dresser
Price checker
Budgeting
Comparison shopper
Store critic
bagger
Cart return
Online shopping
Visit shopping mall
Car shopping
Discount coupons
Make shopping bags
Catalogue shopping
Shopping spree

SOCCER

Coach
Field maintenance
Tournament
Teams
Time keeper
Out of town trips
Referee
Goalie
Team player
World cup
Equipment manager
Goal keeper
Learn rules
Water boy
Travel to England
Soccer scrap book
Soccer coach
English leagues
Watch soccer on TV
Computer games
Goal judge
Collect cards
Statistic keeper
Sponsorship
Spectator
Volunteer
St Johns ambulance
Sell equipment
Fund raising
Half time show
Disabled soccer
Community teams
Security
Soccer league stats
Indoor soccer
Practice soccer drills
Soccer jerseys
History of soccer

SOCIALIZING

Online chat groups
Social groups
Lounge
Parties
Any type of club or group
Health club
Sports clubs
Running clubs
Birthdays
Volunteering
Weddings
Church organization
Showers
Pen pal
Volunteer
Companion
Weight loss
Greeter at store or airport
Attending dances
Training pets
Singles clubs
Hiking club
Bicycle club
Travel clubs
Fishing clubs
Movie club
Boxing club
Martial arts club
Kennel club
Ship model club
Train model club
Plane model club
Support groups
Coffee groups

TRUCKS

Attend car shows
Work with truck mechanic
Build model trucks
Read truck books
Attend a 4x4 show'n'shine
Mud bogging
Visit speedway track
Research different trucks
Visit truck dealership
Work at truck stop
Visit truck garage
Sell trucks
Moving truck business
Truck rental business
Diesel trucks
Commercial trucks
Flatbed trucks
Fire trucks
4x4 trucks
Catering truck
Delivery truck
Boom trucks
Lift trucks
Truck magazines
Die cast truck models
Refurbish vintage trucks
Racing trucks
Vintage trucks

WATER ACTIVITIES

Canoeing
Spring water delivery
Garden pond project
Fishing
Paddle boats
Water treatment plant
Hot tub and spa sales
Watering plants in garden
Marine biology
Model ship building
Pool maintenance
Aquarium care
River rafting
Ornamental ponds
Evaluating lakes
Dam control
Waterfalls
Work at car wash
Fish hatchery
Dragon boat racing
Sailing
Kayaking
Water skiing
Swimming
Wet land conservation

CONNECTING WITH OUR PLANET - MOTHER NATURE

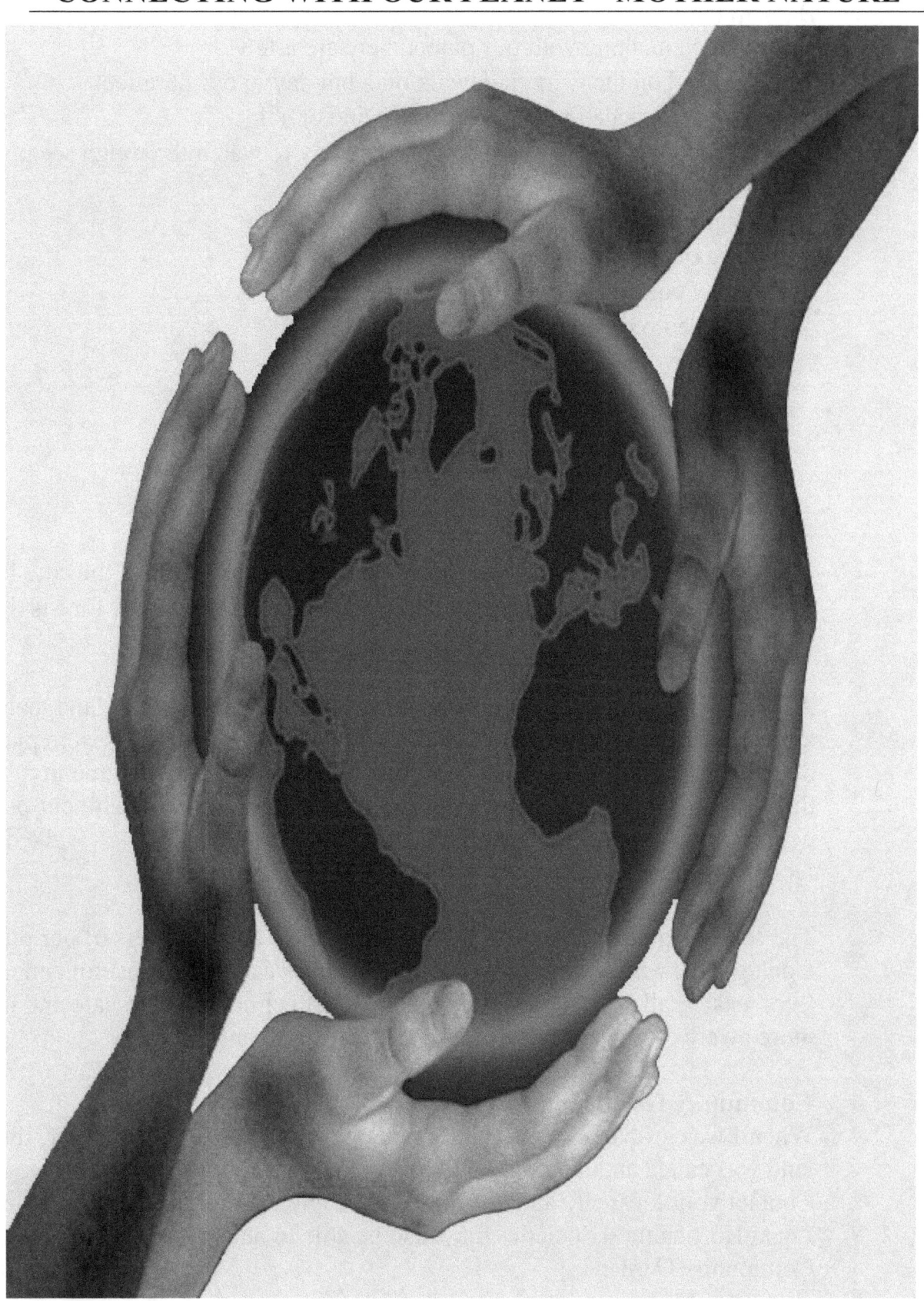

CONNECTING CHILDREN WITH MOTHER NATURE

Back in the fifties when I was growing up, we did things that just seemed natural to connecting with our planet, here are a few:
- Walked on the warm sidewalk on a hot day in our bare feet.
- Played outside in the rain, snow, wind or shine.
- Went down to the beach on a stormy day to watch the rough sea pound the seashore.
- Walked on beach sand in our bare feet.
- Dug our hands in the dirt.
- Grew our own vegetables.
- Weeded our garden.
- Had a compost pile in the garden.
- Collected rain water for the garden plants.
- Pruned our hedge and garden plantings.
- Climbed the hills and sat for hours watching the horizon.
- Played community group games.
- Lay in the grass and watched the clouds.
- Picked mushrooms in the forest, and giant mushrooms in the cow field.
- Explored the community, hills, rocks, cliffs, caves, fields, forests, beach, seashore and played in the sea.

As you can see, I grew up on the shores of the North Sea in England, nature was a natural part of growing up. Then TV came along and less kids were playing outside; it was becoming more difficult to find kids to play community games; the weather became less enjoyable, something that interfered with our plans; less people were outdoors, and people would think you strange if you walked in bare feet or lay in the grass.

The following activities are to help children have an awareness of our planet. Don't get me wrong, electro mechanical devices can be very useful and make our lives easier; all I am suggesting is that we help children appreciate and become more aware of the planet we are on; Mother Earth and nature.

Community Gardening
When I was growing up, my father rented a plot of land from the city, the plot of land was called an allotment, and the land was used to grow our own vegetables. Contact your local city and see if they have any Community Garden plots. Local Horticultural Societies may also be able to help guide you to local Community Gardens.

BENEFITS OF GROWING AND GARDENING

- Access to fresh foods.
- A retreat from concrete environments.
- Children and adults eat healthier meals.
- Food is less likely to have pesticides and is more organic.
- Children get more exercise.
- Motivates children to have an awareness of nature.
- Place to gather and socialize.
- A place for multi-cultural interaction.
- Add nature and beauty to the neighborhood.
- Children learn to care, create and grow a garden.
- Children learn responsibility, cooperation, science, math and other skills.
- Reduces stress and increases a sense of community and belonging.

Home Gardening
Home gardening can be as simple as tending to a plant in a pot.
Check out the local home and garden show.

Benefits:
- Promotes a connection with nature.
- Brings joy, comfort and relaxation.
- Brings satisfaction watching a plant or vegetable mature and grow.

Play with Dirt and Sand
You don't have to be a gardener; many playgrounds have a sand pit or dirt patches; you can buy a bag of soil or sand and just run your fingers through it; or put a slit in the bag of soil and grow some plants and vegetables.

Connecting to the Earth
When you have circle-time ask the children to look outside, notice the trees, the sky, grass, soil, everything in your neighborhood. When you step outside ask the children to consciously connect with the environment.

Connecting with Our Planet
Take off your shoes and walk in the grass; walk on soil or mud; find some rocks and walk on them with bare feet; this May help with balance and has many other benefits. Always check for sharp objects before children take their shoes off. Become conscious of the air you breath; listen to nature sounds, birds, the wind, running water. Go for nature walks, nature trails, parks; watching the animals and birds.

How To Deal With Children's Behaviors

HOW TO DEAL WITH CHILDREN'S BEHAVIORS

Introduction:
Paul Mackie, a professional Early Childhood Educator, reveals effective ways of dealing with pre-school children's behaviors.

Paul has worked in day cares and the school system using Educational Child's Play (simple movements and play based activities that improve children's ability to learn) methods successfully to help children in their development.

Paul has presented seminars on Brain Gym and techniques to reduce stress to both educators and businesses such as Early Childhood Educators of BC, Supported Childcare, The Learning Academy, Crestbrook Forest Industries and others.

My credentials and experience are in the areas of daycares; pre-schools; after school programs; Teachers Assistant in Elementary school and Junior High school; Crisis Line worker; Community Care Worker; experience with Autism, FAS, ADD, ADHD, and working with medium to severe behaviorally and physically challenged children and adults.

Cautions
This information is for educational purposes only. I am not a doctor and would recommend seeking a doctor's, or health professional's advice; if any type of behavior is a problem for you; you can also do a web search for the type of behavior you are dealing with.

I accept no responsibility for any outcomes, or misuse of some of the techniques and methods presented in this book.

Some children's behaviors can be serious and may require medical, or professional help.

My hope is that the knowledge contained in this section will give you enough information to make informed choices when dealing with children's behaviors.

Developmental Milestones

Age	Motor	Speech	Vision and hearing	Social development
4-6 weeks				Smiles at parent
6-8 weeks		Vocalizes		
3 months	Prone: head held up for prolonged periods. No grasp reflex	Makes vowel noises	Follows dangling toy from side to side. Turns head round to sound	Squeals with pleasure appropriately. Discriminates smile
5 months	Holds head steady. Goes for objects and gets them. Objects taken to mouth	Enjoys vocal play		Smiles at mirror image
6 months	Transfers objects from one hand to the other. Pulls self-up to sit and sits erect. Rolls over prone to supine. Palmer grasp of cube	Double syllable sounds such as 'mumum' and 'dada'	Localizes sound 45cm lateral to either ear	May show 'stranger shyness'
9-10 months	Wiggles and crawls. Sits unsupported. Picks up objects with pincer grasp	Babbles tunefully	Looks for toys dropped	Apprehensive about strangers
1 year	Stands holding furniture. Stands alone for a second or two, then collapses with a bump	Babbles 2 or 3 words repeatedly	Drops toys, and watches where they go	Cooperates with dressing, waves goodbye, understands simple commands
18 months	Can walk alone. Picks up toy without falling over. Gets up/down stairs holding onto rail. Begins to jump with both feet. Can build a tower of 3 or 4 cubes and throw a ball	'Jargon'. Many intelligible words		Demands constant mothering. Drinks from a cup with both hands. Feeds self with a spoon
2 years	Able to run. Walks up and down stairs 2 feet per step. Builds tower of 6 cubes	Joins 2-3 words in sentences		Parallel play. Dry by day
3 years	Goes up stairs 1 foot per step and downstairs 2 feet per step. Copies circle, imitates cross and draws man on request. Builds tower of 9 cubes	Constantly asks questions. Speaks in sentences		Cooperative play. Undresses with assistance. Imaginary companions
4 years	Goes down stairs one foot per step, skips on one foot. Imitates gate with cubes, copies a cross	Questioning at its height. Many infantile substitutions in speech		Dresses and undresses with assistance. Attends to own toilet needs
5 years	Skips on both feet and hops. Draws a man and copies a triangle. Gives age	Fluent speech with few infantile substitutions in speech		Dresses and undresses alone
6 years	Copies a diamond shape.	Fluent speech		Knows right from left

A METHOD TO DEAL WITH MOST CHILDREN'S BEHAVIORS

Harm to self, others, or property will dictate how you react.
- Calm yourself first and don't raise your voice.
- Describe the unacceptable behavior to the child.
- Focus on what you want to happen and tell the child.
- Keep your words to a minimum depending on the child's age and cognitive level.
- Give a consequence for the behavior and follow through.

One of the main keys to dealing with children's behaviors is: CONTROLLING EMOTIONS; not theirs, but yours!

So, how do you remain calm, in control and effectively deal with a pre-school child's behavior?

One simple technique is to bend your knees. Most people's legs are locked when they are tense; all you must do is bend your knees.

Stop! Focus on your breathing; breath in through your nose and out through your mouth; expand your stomach as you breath in.

Cross your hands under your armpits, put your tongue on the roof of your mouth and breath into your stomach. Tell yourself, "I am calm and can handle this".

Some activities to help beat stress are:
Breathing
Balance Board
Creative Thinking
Energizing the Body
Meditation
Moving to Relax
Relaxation Activities
Sensory Environment
Visualization
Personal creative time (very important)

AVOIDING BURN OUT

IT IS VITAL THAT YOU MAKE TIME FOR YOURSELF.

DO SOMETHING CREATIVE FOR YOURSELF.

DO NOT BRING YOUR WORK HOME WITH YOU.

USE THIS BOOK'S TECHNIQUES AND ACTIVITIES ON A DAILY BASIS.

DO A 10 MINUTE MEDITATION WHEN YOU GET HOME FROM WORK.

IF YOU ARE PUTTING 110% INTO YOUR JOB - STOP!

SOME COMMON BEHAVIORS IN PRE-SCHOOL CHILDREN

A child may hold their breath: as far as I know from my First Aid training, a child cannot choke, or stop themselves breathing. If they do become unconscious, they will start breathing automatically. This can be a terrifying situation, usually the child can go bright red, purple, or blue; collapse and look like they are having a seizure;
usually they will start breathing within a minute; possibly cry or be tired.

Temper Tantrums: Tantrums are typical for children between the ages of fifteen months and three years. Don't give in; giving in to a child when they are having a temper tantrum will only guarantee there will be more tantrums.
Calm yourself first and then the child.
Take several deep breaths before you speak.
Usually the child is wanting or objecting to a change you have asked the child to do.
Describe to the child what you see the child doing.
Once the tantrum has stopped, switch the focus from whatever the child wants, and re-direct giving two positive choices; "I see you are calm now, would you like to read a book, or join our story time"?

Hitting-Hurting and Damaging Property: If a child is hurting or hitting someone, deal with the hurt child first, then the child doing the hitting.

Keep in mind: Pre-school children are testing their limits and boundaries, a normal part of child growth.

How to deal with a child's behavior - Certain behaviors are age appropriate.

- Talk about what is happening in the moment.
- Focus on what you want a child to do-not on what you don't want them to do.
- A child misbehaving is a form of communication-what is the child trying to say?
- Define the behavior - what is the child doing that you don't like?
- Tell the child in short two or three word sentences - "Hitting hurts".
- Give a consequence for the behavior, "If you keep hitting the other children, I will call your parents"; follow through if you give a consequence.
- Re-direct giving two positive choices; "Would you like to do this, or that"? You are not rewarding the child, just re-directing to another activity.
- Communication is key with a pre-school child; "say what you mean and mean what you say." Always follow through, and explain what you are doing, and why you are doing it.
- Treat children with respect and empathy.
- Talk about feelings-yours and theirs.
- Providing balance activities can help; see the Story Mat, Balance Board, vestibular and Proprioceptive activities.
- Set limits and hold the child accountable for their actions.
- Give lots of praise when children are doing the right thing.
- Always ask before you touch a child. If you must restrain a child, have a witness present; **a last resort for harm to self or others by a child.**

Building Self Esteem in Children
- Treat children with respect and always talk to them at their level.
- Encourage and focus on a child's interests and strengths.
- Have expectations that are age appropriate.
- Show children they are appreciated and loved.
- Give lots of praise, even for the small day to day things.
- Be gentle and reasonable; firm-discipline is not punishment, it is guidance.
- Model the behavior you expect from children through understanding and communication.
- Use positive reinforcement to reward proper behavior.
- Give children choices.
- Be consistent.

WHAT HAPPENS WHEN NONE OF THIS WORKS?

The following is a story of how I started using the Balance Board with a troubled child and reached a point where I was about to give up its use, when an amazing thing happened.

Several years ago, I was hired by a daycare to work with a three year old boy who had severe behavioral problems. As an Early Childhood Educator who had some experience working with behaviorally challenged children I thought, "How bad could it be?" After all, he was only three years old.

Tommy (not his real name) knew a lot of words; he favored "F _ _ _ You!" followed by a string of two to three word sentences of the same language.
At first, I tried the usual methods of behavioral management such as time-out, transitional methods (timers, communication of changes in activities etc.), rewards and praise for good behavior, but all to no avail. It was at this point that I decided to use a new approach, new to me anyway; this was to use a wonderful piece of equipment called a Balance Board.

The techniques of the Balance Board Program which I had learned did not fit with this situation, so I decided to change the method into a play-based routine.

I introduced Tommy to the Rotational Balance Board.
I started by taking Tommy to the staff room which was large, open and free of distractions. At first, I just sat on the Balance Board and spun around a few times; then I asked Tommy to do the same. Tommy tried it, quickly got bored, and then started jumping on the staff room furniture and pulling pictures off the walls. I persevered.

With all this spinning I would get dizzy. Tommy found this to be funny and would stop his negative behaviors to come over and laugh at me! I would hold my head, groaning, and tell him I felt sick. It became a game for Tommy, giving me a clue about how to reach him.

Tommy started using the board. The first thing I noticed was that Tommy did not get dizzy; he would spin for five minutes, get up off the board and walk away (I later found out this could be a possible indicator that a person may have sensory difficulties). Another thing was his awareness of where he was in space; he would run his hand along the wall all the time (another possible indicator of sensory difficulties) and would slide on his back on the floor, bumping his head quite hard on walls, doors and furniture.

When Tommy was used to the daily routine of five minutes on the rotational board, I introduced the Rocking Balance Board. The method for the use of this board is to stand perfectly balanced (adjustable rockers can increase the level of balance difficulty) while carrying out certain hand/eye coordination activities (hitting targets, catching balls etc.).

I had Tommy stand on the Rocking Balance Board and throw a soft bean bag at my stomach.
Whenever he would hit my stomach dead-on, I would bend over and say, "Ow! that hurt." If he missed and hit some other part of my body I would not react as much; the more I reacted, the more he hit the target and the louder he would laugh.

Tommy's behaviors had decreased a little and he was swearing less, but after two months, I began to doubt whether the balance board activities were having much effect. It was at this point that an amazing thing happened.

One day after our usual five minutes of spinning Tommy stood up and said, "I feel dizzy;" something had changed, which was not amazing in itself; the truly amazing thing happened the next day.

The next day I was watching as a boy took Tommy's train set; I quickly stepped in to prevent Tommy from snatching back the train and hitting the boy as he typically would. To my surprise, Tommy came over to me and said, "He has taken my train!" I asked Tommy, "What should we do about that?" Tommy replied, "He took my train set. Let's go and ask for it back!" (twelve words, in sentences – truly amazing for this little boy). I helped Tommy get the train back by using his words.

From that point on, Tommy's use of vocabulary increased dramatically. He could communicate his needs and feelings and his violent outbursts decreased. Tommy still had behaviors, but more at the level of a developing three year old.

Another interesting thing was that Tommy stopped running his hands on the walls, although he would still slide on the floor. He would however slow down and gently touch his head to objects instead of hitting them hard.

I have used Balance Board activities with:
- Babies, by holding them in a sitting position on the board.
- Pre-school children, as part of my storybook activity.
- With school children and college students studying for tests.
- Special needs adults and the elderly; they all seemed to enjoy the activities.

There are some safety issues when using the Balance Board which I discuss in the Balance Board section of this book.

I personally use the board daily to help center and focus myself before the day starts.

The activities in this book can be printed and placed on the wall as a reminder of what to do.

Dealing with children's behaviors daily can be challenging, but providing a safe, sensory rich, play based environment can be helpful for the care giver and the child.

DEALING WITH EMOTIONS

It is important that pre-school children begin to understand their own basic emotions.

Emotions and opposites
Sad   Happy
Angry Calm
Hurt   Well

The three emotions above and their opposite emotion pictures can be placed around the room.

Circle Time discussions about feelings and why the pictures are different, can be discussed with children.

Children under two will not be able to express their emotions, but activities and stories about emotions should be introduced between the ages of two and six years of age.

I have included pictures of opposite emotions that can be printed and placed on walls for show and tell; or discuss during Circle Time.

Body and basic sign language can be used as visual cues instead of words, when
dealing with a child's behavior. Constant use of basic sign, body language, and words will help children communicate easier.

The following pictures of emotions and basic sign language can be printed and placed on walls around the room.

If you do have to say "NO" always explain why.

As mentioned before: Focus on what you want a child to do - not on what you don't want them to do.

SAD FACE

HAPPY FACE

ANGRY FACE

CALM FACE

HURT FACE

WELL FACE

BASIC SIGN LANGUAGE - YES

HAND MOVES UP AND DOWN

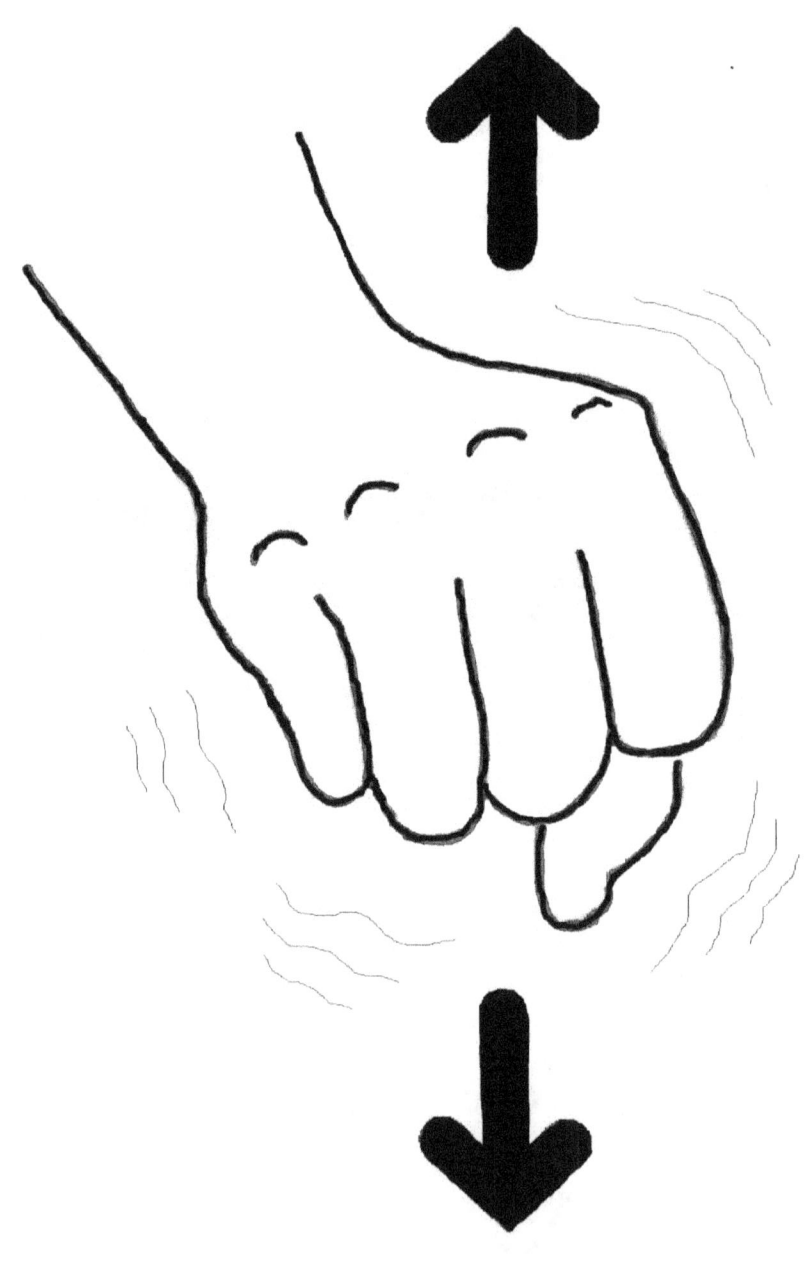

BASIC SIGN LANGUAGE - NO

FINGERS TOUCH TOGETHER

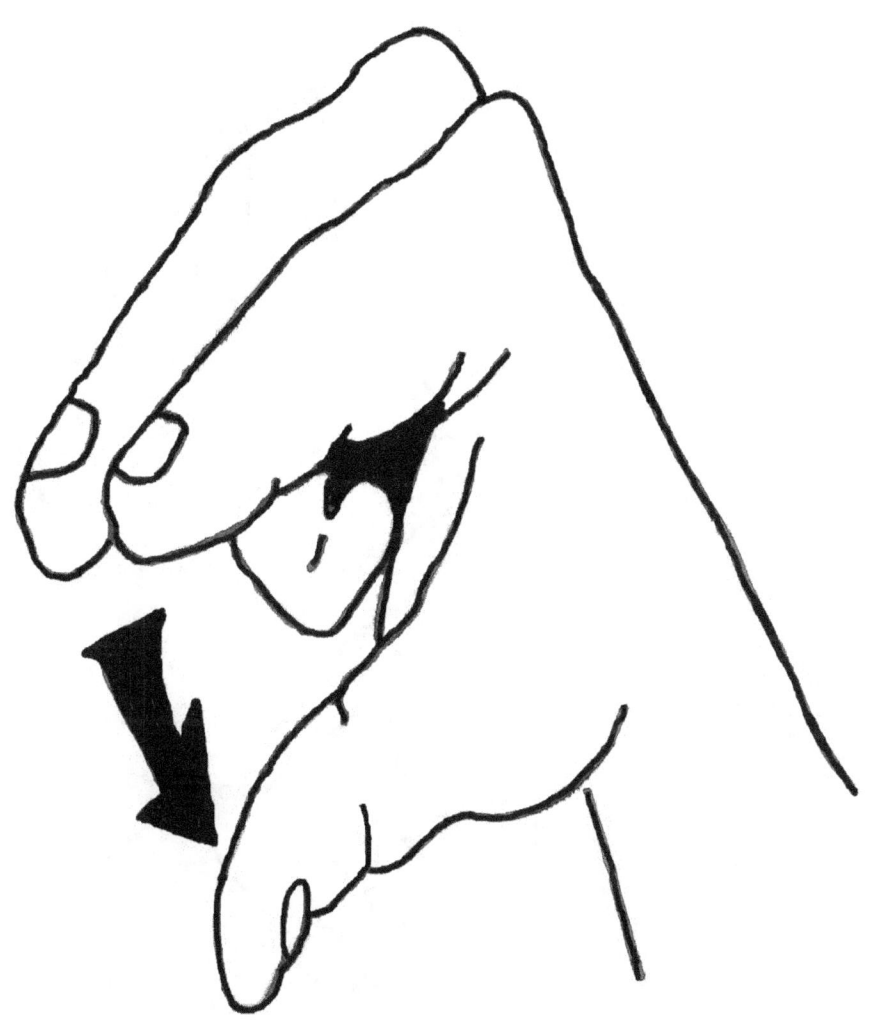

BASIC SIGN LANGUAGE - STOP

HANDS TOUCH TOGETHER

BASIC SIGN LANGUAGE
BATHROOM - TOILET

LETTER "T" SHAKE HAND

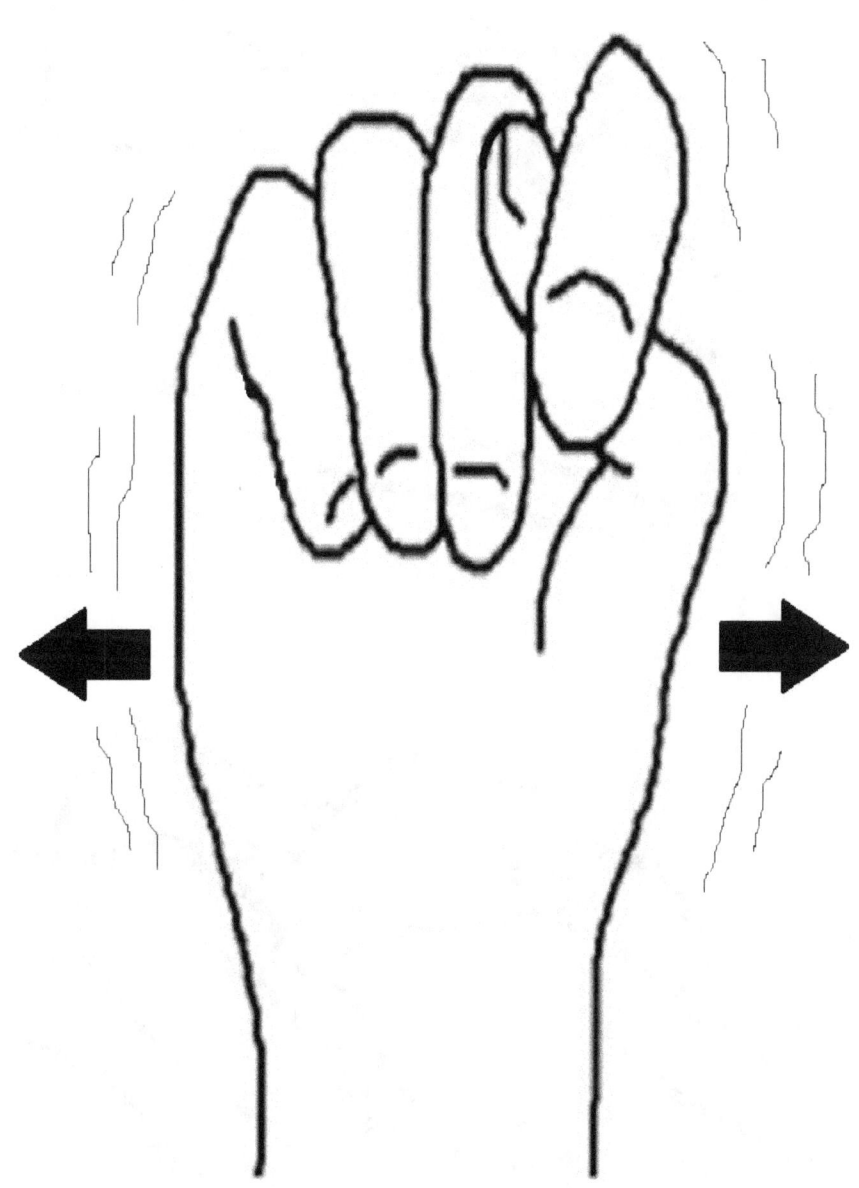

BASIC SIGN LANGUAGE – STORY TIME

HANDS ARE CLOSED THEN OPENED LIKE A BOOK

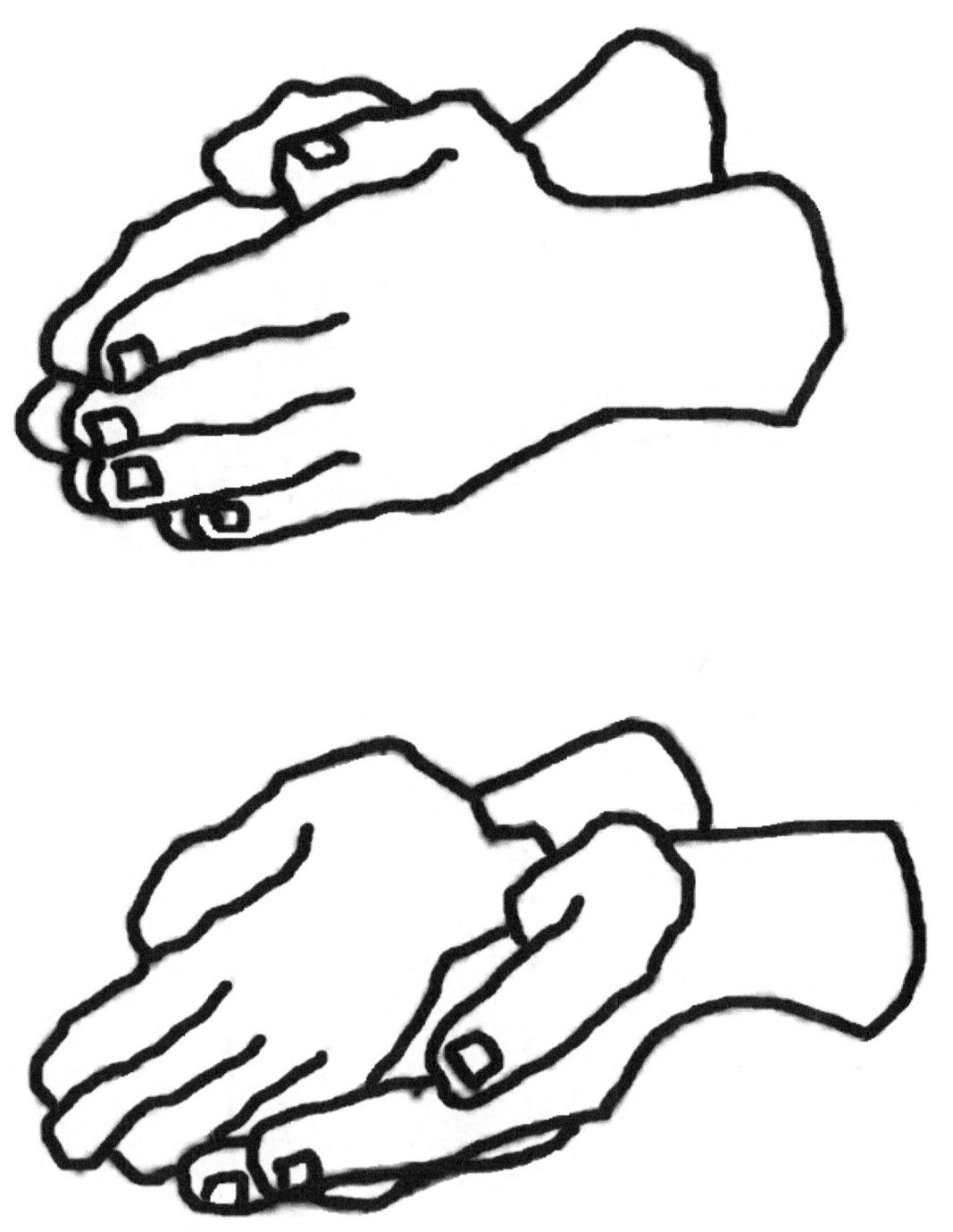

BASIC SIGN LANGUAGE –
EAT - HUNGRY

FINGERS GO TO MOUTH AS IF EATING

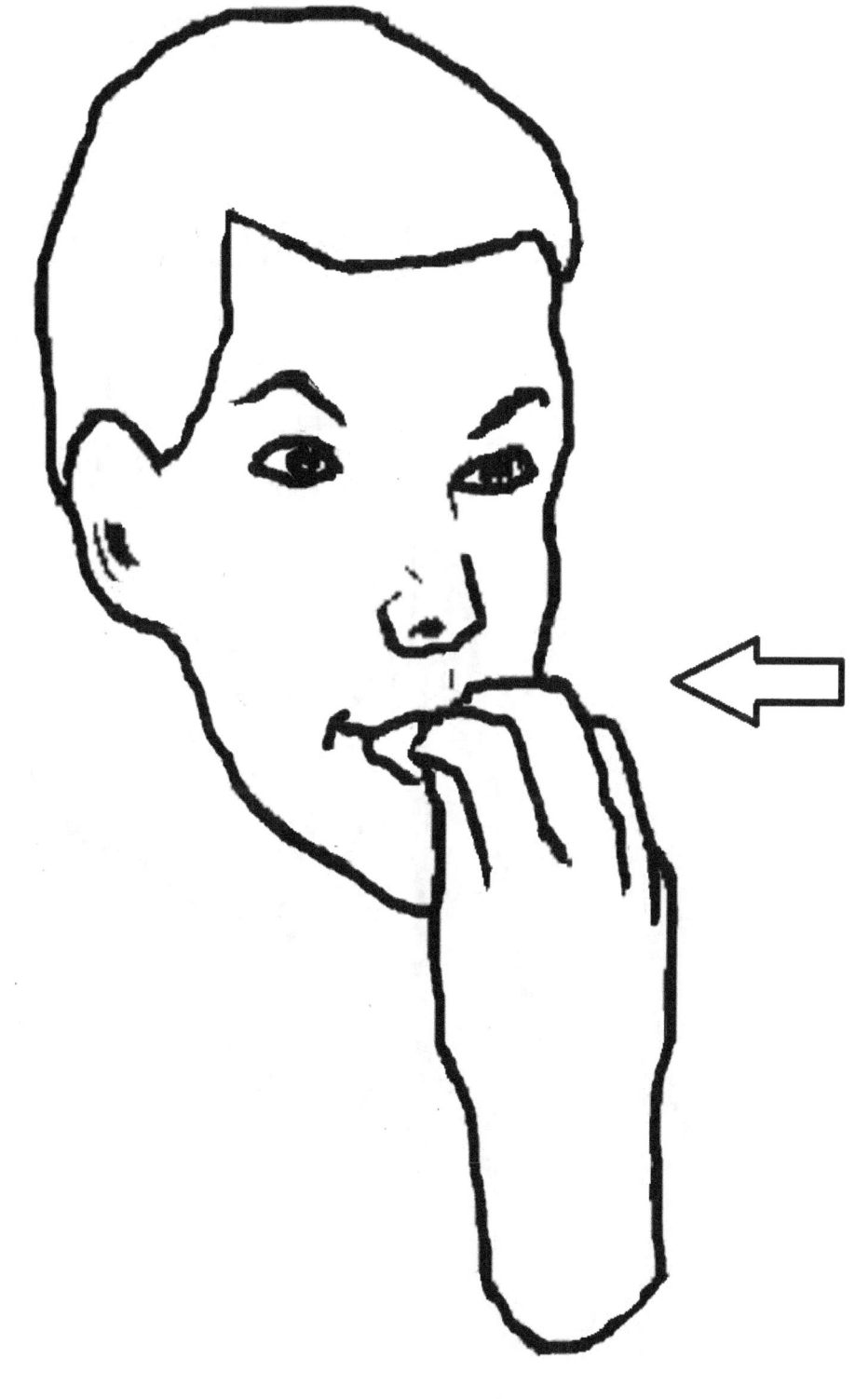

Basic Sign Language –
SLEEP - NAP TIME

HANDS TOGETHER AND GO TO SIDE OF FACE

FOR THOSE THAT WANT TO KNOW MORE

About this book
This book contains a series of activities which are said to help child development.
Activities are presented as stories and play based activity centers.

Educational Child's Play is as easy as ABC.
A. Choose one or more activities from the Educational Child's Play book.
B. Set-up the activity as a center or table top activity.
C. Let children explore the activities. **IT'S THAT EASY!**

What is Educational Child's Play?
"Educational Child's Play" stresses self-direction, self-motivation and self-exploration; and be supported by the parent or teacher when needed.

"Educational Child's Play" is cooperative play which promotes communication and cooperation with others, in an activity of discovery.

"Educational Child's Play" promotes the ability for children to think for themselves, communicate and talk openly about their experiences, feelings and ideas.

"Educational Child's Play" is presented before seven years of age, to help develop a rich network of neural pathways that permit complex thinking.

"Educational Child's Play" can be presented by parents as home based activities; a supplemental before and after school daycare program, or a series of fun developmental activities.

Most parents, daycares, preschools and after-school programs generally offer play based activities, with some daily structure, and activities like the list below. Art and Crafts, Blocks, Books, Computer and Software Programs, Dramatic Play, Games, Musical Toys and Instruments, Physical Education Equipment, Playground Equipment, Science Activities, Stacking Toys, small building toys (Lego), Other toys.
The above list represents good quality activities, but a vital part is missing.

"Educational Child's Play" is based on what scientists are saying children need in the first seven years of life, when the base for competence and coping skills that will affect learning, behavior and health throughout life is formed.
Many professional teachers are also suggesting that children should have a less structured school environment, where they are free to explore and develop the abilities and talents that they are good at.

WHAT CAN EDUCATIONAL CHILD'S PLAY DO FOR A CHILD?

Educational Child's Play is a series of developmental and fun activities. It is hoped that the activities will develop a child's cognitive, behavioral, emotional and motor skills.

Unfortunately, there are no guarantees; the possible outcomes are based on the author's own experiences and observed results of children in the author's care; it is hoped that you can achieve the same results.

The concept of this book's activities is to help children:

- Develop the Brain's neural pathways.
- Socialize and get to know each other.
- Learn how to handle stress and emotions.
- Learn how to participate in group activities.
- Have better communication and thinking skills.

Possible Outcomes

Cognitive
- Increased cognition and thinking skills.
- Increased self-direction.
- Enhanced ability to sequence information.
- Increased ability to problem solve

Behavioral
- Increased motivation.
- Increased organizational skills.
- Enthusiasm to learn.

Emotional
- Overcoming the effects of emotional stress
- Increased emotional self-control.
- Increased self-esteem.
- Increased social skills, confidence and cooperation.

Motor Skills
- Improved coordination.
- Greater sense of rhythm and balance.
- Increase visual and auditory processing.

FROM THE ONTARIO EARLY YEARS FRAMEWORK REPORT

With Ontario leading the way, the Council of Ministers of Education endorses play-based learning

The Council of Ministers of Education believes that purposeful, play-based early learning sets the stage for future learning, health, and well-being. In the Council of Ministers of Education Statement on Play-Based Learning (2012), the council describes the benefits of play, as recognized by the scientific community, early learning experts, and children and families alike.

Learning through play is supported by science

- Scientific evidence demonstrates that neural pathways in the brains of children are built through the exploration, thinking, problem solving, and language expression that occur during play.

Learning through play is supported by experts

- Experts such as Lev Vygotsky identify play as a leading source of social, emotional, physical, language, and cognitive development. Intentional play-based learning allows children to investigate, ask questions, solve problems, and engage in critical thinking.

Learning through play is supported by children and families

- Children themselves are naturally driven to play, and early learning through play often takes the form of manipulating objects, acting out roles, and experimenting with different materials.
- Parents also understand that play is valuable to development, allowing children to construct, challenge, and expand their understanding of the world around them.

OTHER BOOKS BY THE AUTHOR

http://www.lulu.com/spotlight/paulmackie
https://www.amazon.com/-/e/B0713QH79J

	**EDUCATIONAL CHILD'S PLAY** Play Based Child Development Activities. Prepare pre-school children emotionally, intellectually and physically, before they start school. A book jammed packed with play based child development activities.
	**WORKPLACE STRESS MANAGEMENT** Do you feel stressed and anxious at work? You're about to discover easy to do workplace stress management activities to reduce stress, anxiety, and the possibility of a nervous breakdown in the workplace. You will Learn: a 5-minute exercise to start and finish your day; practical, easy to learn movements to help reduce workplace stress.
	**PRE SCHOOL COLORING AND PUZZLE BOOK** This coloring book is designed to help pre-school children with the following possible benefits: increase creativity; a free time activity; a transitional activity; a soothing distraction; improve fine motor skills; calm and center the mind; stimulate the brain and the senses; help focus the mind in the moment; take the mind off distracting thoughts.
	**FUN DAY FOR SENIORS** Thousands of activities to help seniors be alert, in the moment, energized and living a full life.

	**A WALK IN THE JUNGLE** Prepare preschool children emotionally, intellectually and physically, before they go to grade school. Give your child an unprecedented, LIFELONG advantage, simply by reading them a storybook; a storybook UNLIKE ANY OTHER you've seen before. It feels so good to see your child achieve milestones, absorb knowledge like a sponge and develop a true love of learning.
	LEO READS TO LEARN Leo Reads To Learn How to teach the fundamentals of reading This storybook helps children learn the fundamental keys to reading, and gives children the exciting gift, that they are "Reading to Learn".
	**ADULT AND CHILDREN COLORING BOOK** A 128 page adult and children coloring and puzzle book. The pictures and puzzles are printable for any age group, from adult coloring to children. This book was designed for my 42 year old daughter who had a stroke and has limited movement and communication due to her stroke. This book is helping her use both hands, better her fine motor skills, and improve logical thinking skills.
	**MOTIVATIONAL COLORING PUZZLE BOOK** This book has inspirational pictures, comic art, and puzzles for children, adults and seniors. It is the Author's hope readers may experience some of the following benefits: Give children a calming activity. Help children learn to read and write. Increase your creativity. Challenge your thinking skills. Reduce stress. Improve your state of wellness. Improve fine motor skills. Calm and center the mind in the moment.

GETTING THROUGH YOUR DAY
Getting Through Your Day Motivational Activities to help you reduce stress, be alert, in the moment, energized, and living a full life. This book introduces you to a 5-minute movement based exercise to start your day. You will learn to focus the mind, energize the body, and be ready for a meaningful day.

GORDY VISITS THE MOUTAINS
Gordy Visits The Mountains: helps children develop physical coordination, improves self-direction, enhances decision making, promotes problem solving. A fun play-based child development storybook activity gets your child ready to learn.

HOW TO TEACH CHILDREN TO READ
This book introduces children to 86 phonetic sounds of the English language in a step by step plan to teach a child of any age to read. How To Teach Children To Read also introduces the 220 Dolch word list (sight words) so that a child will be able to read, write and spell most written words.

ALPHABET PARK
This story is designed to teach children the basics of reading; so, they will learn to read, and "read to learn".
The Alphabet Park story teaches preschool children the sounds of the alphabet; that each letter has different sounds; those sounds make words; the beginning of phonetics; and the Whole Word method of reading.

TEACH YOUR CHILD TO READ COLORING BOOK
This book is a coloring book with a combination of coloring book pages from How To Teach Children To Read, Alphabet Park and other activities that introduce children to the Alphabet sounds (phonetics) and sight words needed to be able to read and write most written words.

BIBLIOGRAPHY

Smart Moves by Carla Hannaford, Ph.D. ISBN 0-915556-26-X
Why learning is not all in the head.

Creative Play for the Developing Child by Clare Cherry. ISBN-0-8224-1632-8
A book that illuminates the value of play in relation to child development during the first few years of life.

Is the Left Brain Always Right? by Clare Cherry. ISBN-0-8224-3911-5
A guide to whole brain development. This book demonstrates the need for educational programs that develop the whole child. It also shows you how to create appropriate activities and learning opportunities.

Creative Movement for the Developing Child by Clare Cherry. ISBN-0-8224-1660-3
A book to develop sensory perception during the various stages of a child's growth.

Aromatherapy Workbook by Marcel Lavabre ISBN-0-89281-346-6
A book that explores why and how to use aromatic oils.

Fundamentals Guidebook by Gordon Dryden & Colin Rose ISBN-0-905553-44-6
Part of an educational kit of activities to raise a brighter happier child.

Kindergarten Maximum Stimulation by Lyelle Palmer
A book for researchers to improve young children's learning abilities.

The Hug Therapy Book: by Kathleen Keating
Explains the positive results of how and why you should hug.

The Throwing Madonna by Dr. William Calvin
Dr. Calvin puts forward the theory that throwing and running on large rocks led humans to develop bigger brains.

Facial Expressions
https://commons.wikimedia.org/wiki/Category:Line_drawings_of_facial_expressions

Ontario Early Years Framework
http://www.edu.gov.on.ca/childcare/OntarioEarlyYear.pdf

ABOUT THE AUTHOR

The author (Paul Mackie) has over twenty years of experience working with children and adults as an educator, and personal care worker.

Paul is a certified Early Childhood Educator in British Columbia, and a level two Early Childhood educator in Alberta Canada.

Paul has worked as a Community Care worker with special needs children, adults and seniors; and has worked with children in Daycares, Day Programs, and the School System.

The author has had several careers, with certification as a Marine Engineer; Industrial Millwright, Welder; Early Childhood Educator; with experience as a Teacher's Assistant; Special Needs Childcare Worker; Brain Gym Instructor; Senior Building Manager; with courses of study such as "The writing Road to Reading", "Accelerated Learning" and other Brain development courses.

The author is now retired from his last position as Senior Building Manager for a non-profit housing society.

Visit: http://howtoteachchildrentoread.ca/

https://www.amazon.com/-/e/B0713QH79J

Please feel free to leave a review on Amazon or Contact me at: educationalchildsplay@gmail.com

Have a great day.
Paul Mackie